The English Reformation 1530–1570

W. J. Sheils

LONGMAN
London and New York

Addison Wesley Longman Limited
Edinburgh Gate, Harlow,
Essex CM20 2JE, England
and Associated Companies throughout the world.

Published in the United States of America
by Addison Wesley Longman Inc., New York.

First published in 1989
Eighth impression 1998

Set in 10/11 point Baskerville (Linotron)

Printed in Malaysia

ISBN 0 582 35398 X

British Library Cataloguing in Publication Data
Sheils, W. J. (William J.)
    The English Reformation: 1530–1570.
    1. England. Christian Church. Reformation,
    1509–1570
    I. Title   II. Series
    274.2'06

        ISBN 0-582-35398-X

The publisher's policy is to use paper manufactured from sustainable forests.

Library of Congress Cataloging-in-Publication Data
Sheils, W. J.
    The English Reformation, 1530–1570.

    (Seminar studies in history)
    Bibliography: p.
    Includes index.
    1. Reformation—England.   2. England—Church
history—16th century.   I. Title.   II. Series.
    BR375.S49   1989   274.2'06   88-13023
    ISBN 0-582-35398-X

Contents

Contents

Seminar Studies in History

Introduction

The Seminar Studies series was conceived by Patrick Richardson, whose experience of teaching history persuaded him of the need for something more substantial than a textbook chapter but less formidable than the specialised full-length academic work. He was also convinced that such studies, although limited in length, should provide an up-to-date authoritative introduction to the topic under discussion as well as a selection of relevant documents and a comprehensive bibliography.

Patrick Richardson died in 1979, but by that time the Seminar Studies series was firmly established, and it continues to fulfil the role he intended for it. This book, like others in the series, is therefore a living tribute to a gifted and original teacher.

Note on the System of References:
A bold number in round brackets (**5**) in the text refers the reader to the corresponding entry in the Bibliography section at the end of the book. If a name follows the bold number, this is the author of a particular essay in a collection. A bold number in square brackets, preceded by 'doc.' [**doc. 6**] refers the reader to the corresponding item in the section of Documents, which follows the main text.

Acknowledgements

We are grateful to the following for permission to reproduce copyright material:

Cambridge University Press for an extract from *The Tudor Constitution* by G. R. Elton pp. 416–8 and the Folger Institute at the Folger Shakespeare Library for extracts from *An Apology to the Church of England By John Jewel*, ed. J. E. Booty, pubd. Cornell University Press 1963.

Part One: Introduction

1 The State of the Church

Demands for reform

It has often been said that the Reformation changes of the 1530s amounted to an Act of State. No doubt the changes brought about by the Reformation Parliament reflected the determination of Crown, government and landed classes to reduce both the political power and landed wealth of the late medieval Church. This determination was given urgency by the King's inability to secure Papal support for the annulment of his marriage to Catherine of Aragon, a marriage which had failed to produce the male heir thought necessary by Henry VIII to secure the Tudor dynasty. These motives were important springs to action, but even a government led by an administrator as able as Thomas Cromwell would not have been successful in carrying through its policy if an important sector of society did not share some of its ambitions. Contemporary evidence shows that in the early sixteenth century there was widespread dissatisfaction with the Church as it existed, and that this dissatisfaction was found among all sectors of society (**42**).

In addition to the obvious abuses of wealth which brought criticisms from both landowners envious of monastic and other ecclesiastical estates (**114**), and from peasants caught up in the intricacies of a cumbersome and sometimes expensive legal system, humanist learning had come into England from the Continent and brought with it a new scriptural view of the pastoral role of the Church which, however idealistic, exposed the deficiencies of the clergy to a literate and highly articulate group in society (**80**). Other less influential groups had also been critical of the Church, and throughout the fifteenth century small groups of Lollards, consisting largely of minor landholders and peasants, had continued a fitful and underground heretical tradition which could provide a ready reception for the Lutheran doctrines which began to filter into England during the 1520s (**19, 41, 109**).

Paradoxically, another trend which led to criticism of the Church from some quarters was the resurgence in conventional piety among all sectors of society, which can be traced from the early fifteenth century onwards (**110**). This conventional piety required that the clergy be better able to fulfil their pastoral responsibilities, and it is particularly important in reminding us that the clear call for reform of the Church in the early sixteenth century did not necessarily imply a break with Catholicism. Some people thought that the only way to reform the Church was to restructure it so radically that their policies amounted to wholesale reformation; others, while agreeing that reform was necessary, envisaged a piecemeal adaptation of existing institutions. Finally, it must be remembered that many of the fiercest critics of the Church were themselves clergymen, like William Tyndale (**13**, Tyndale, **84**), and so the Reformation can by no means be explained solely in terms of a conflict between laity and clergy (**37**). Anti-clericalism certainly existed, but it was often motivated by a desire to renew the scriptural role of the clergy and it rarely articulated the demand to destroy the priestly caste *per se*. What it amounted to was a demand for better priests, or different sorts of priests, not for the destruction of the Church or ministry (**126**).

The anti-clerical attitudes among the laity were recognised by a few churchmen as having some justification in fact. The most famous example of this is perhaps the sermon preached by the humanist and biblical scholar John Colet before the assembled Convocation of the province of Canterbury in 1511. This body, the representative assembly of the clergy of the whole archbishopric, had been summoned by Archbishop Warham to consider the problem posed by heresy. Colet, who was Dean of St Paul's, was chosen to preach the opening sermon and, in doing so, placed the blame for ignorance and heresy among the laity squarely on the shoulders of the clergy [**doc. 1**]. There were four fundamental evils which led men away from the Church and brought dishonour on the priesthood: ambition, which led to a scramble for ecclesiastical office and to pluralism; carnal and moral laxity among the clergy; covetousness, which made the clergy greedy and uncharitable in exacting their dues from the laity; and finally, and perhaps most importantly, too great a concern with the affairs of the secular world. To Colet the solution was clear: the Church should reform itself. 'This reformation and restoring of the Church's estate must needs begin of you, our fathers, and so follow in us your priests and in all your clergy . . . It is an old proverb: Physician heal thyself. You spiritual physicians, first taste you this medicine of purgation of manners, and then after offer us the same taste' (**17**).

As a humanist Colet might be expected to represent the new view of the priesthood and to be out of step with more orthodox churchmen. In this case, however, he was reiterating the complaints which had been made by many conscientious clergy about the Church, and his proposed remedies reflected the views expressed by Thomas Bourgchier, Archbishop of Canterbury, in 1455. Men such as these saw the Church as the instrument of its own reformation, but in the early sixteenth century there were others who grew impatient with the Church and demanded that reformation should come from outside the ranks of the clergy. Such men were looking to the godly prince. By the 1530s this sort of reform was associated with the Christian humanists (**48, 80**).

Paradoxically, the humanists often saw the secular arm as being the instrument which would bring about the reform of the Church, the body of Christ. One of their chief inspirations was, of course, Erasmus, whose editions of the New Testament in Greek and Latin were influential in the English universities, where he had spent some time between 1511 and 1514 (**98**). His astringent comments on the religious orders and the excesses of conventional piety dealt a serious blow to the reputation of the medieval Church but, as in the case of his friend Sir Thomas More who was executed for his opposition to the King's divorce, they did not always lead the humanists into acceptance of the Reformation. This dilemma is illustrated by the career of Thomas Starkey, one of the most influential English humanists. After spending some time in Italy in the service of Reginald Pole, later a Cardinal and ultimately the close confidant of Queen Mary, he returned to England in December 1534 and, though he remained a Catholic, Starkey soon identified himself with the policies of Thomas Cromwell. His book in defence of a united Church and State under a constitutional monarch was published in 1536 as *An Exhortation to the people instructing them to unity and obedience*. In this and other writings he was critical of the Church and defended the dissolution of the lesser monasteries, recommending that their income be devoted to educational purposes (**48**). As the century progressed, this type of charitable work, which concerned itself with this world, was to replace the traditional form of medieval piety (**71**) with its concentration on the hereafter. For humanists like Starkey, the reform of the Church was the central feature of a more general plan for the reform of society as a whole. Indeed, he produced such a plan covering social and economic policy from the problem of poverty to the manufacture and sale of woollen cloth. The influence of Starkey and his associates is difficult to assess. Their influence on the formation of policy may have been indirect, but their works certainly provided a vigorous critique of the contemporary Church and society, and their arguments were crucial in creating a climate of opinion which made government policy in the 1530s acceptable to an important part of the political nation (**47, 68**).

These men, whether they sought reform of the Church by the Church like Colet, or reform by the Crown like Starkey, were the intellectuals of the day. Their criticism of the Church found a ready reception among the less high-minded of their contemporaries also and thus these intellectual movements lent support to popular anti-clerical attitudes which had always existed among various sectors of English society. The most striking and famous expression of these was *A Supplication for the Beggars* published by Simon Fish towards the end of the 1520s, a greatly exaggerated but powerful piece of invective against the clergy [**doc. 3**]. Significantly the document was presented as an appeal to the King by the poor and weak members of society to protect them from the evil exactions of greedy clerics. In this way not only did the Church heap sufferings on the poor, but it also rendered the clergy immune from the law and diminished the power of the Crown. Thus the King and the poor shared a common enemy in the Church. That such criticism, in which Henry was advised to 'Tie these holy idle thieves [the priests] to the carts, to be whipped naked about every market town', could find a ready audience and be taken seriously by opponents like John Fisher and Sir Thomas More [**doc. 4**], who wrote a reply to its charges, shows the strength of anti-clerical feeling in some quarters on the eve of the Reformation.

The forcefulness of Fish's claims and his vigorous style have perhaps been too successful, and the early sixteenth-century Church has not had a good reputation among historians. Having shown that there were demands for reform both within and without the Church we should now look briefly at the institution to see how far such criticism was justified. In doing so we can take as our starting point the four crucial failings identified by Colet in his sermon of 1511.

The ills of the Church

The career of Thomas Wolsey, a lowly-born cleric who became Archbishop of York, Cardinal and Papal Legate in addition to occupying several other wealthy church livings which he held along with the chief office of State, the Lord Chancellorship, provided contemporaries with the greatest example of the excesses of ambition. His power, and the manner in which he flaunted it, made many enemies and was a source of scandal (**97**). Wolsey's case was exceptional in scale, but it highlighted the fact that pluralism was an accepted feature of church life. In the localities this led to fundamental flaws in the provision of clergy, the more so because, as in Lancashire, it was usually the richer livings that were held in plurality and a prominent local cleric like Richard Dudley could serve two parishes, Walton and Warton, with a joint income of £144 6*s*. 11*d*. (£144 35p) a year, as well as several cathedral posts. Men like Dudley, who left their parishes to be served by poorly-paid curates while they enjoyed the profits, could be found in every diocese (**55**). In Lincoln diocese between 1514 and 1520 over one-fifth of the parishes were served by such pluralists and, although only eight were deprived of priests entirely, most were served by poorly-paid local men (**24**).

Such men comprised a large proportion of the parish clergy, almost half in the diocese of Canterbury in 1521, and 85 per cent in Hampshire in 1541. Conscientious they may have been, like John Greenwood at Heptonstall, learned they were not, but poor they certainly were. Only 8 of the 295 chaplains in Yorkshire in 1525 had an income greater than £5 a year, and in Staffordshire in 1541 the figure was 9 out of 166. Pluralism represented an unfair division of labour between a minority of very wealthy clergy and a majority of poor men who did most of the parochial work. From this structural flaw, critics maintained, negligence and immorality derived (**62, 60,** Zell).

Immorality, however, only concerned a tiny fraction of priests, but, as with pluralism, the excesses of a few damaged the reputation of all. Scandals like the brothel for clergy in the London parish of St John Zachary were indefensible, but the clergy in general were not promiscuous (**62**). More usual was the case of Alexander Thornton, a Lancashire chantry priest who lived with the same partner, by whom he had a son who also became a priest, from 1489 until 1514 (**55**). Such relationships with 'hearth companions' were defended by the clergy of Bangor diocese in the 1530s as necessary for the provision of that hospitality towards parishioners required of the clergy (**62**). In many areas there was, therefore, a gap between strict law and local custom over the matter of clerical celibacy, but this gap was not due to immorality, nor did it lead to neglect of pastoral work. In his visitations of 266 churches, Archbishop Warham found only eleven cases of such neglect, and a recent study of the huge diocese of Lincoln has concluded 'if chastity was a heavy burden for some, the duties of saying mass and the offices, of hearing confessions and visiting the sick were not, and very few clergy in the diocese failed in their liturgical or pastoral obligations' (**25, 60,** Zell).

Colet's third criticism was of covetousness, referring to the exactions of the Church on the laity. These exactions came about in two ways: as property rights through tithe, the tax levied upon produce for the maintenance of the ministry; and as fees both for spiritual services and, more contentiously, for legal expenses in the church courts. The amounts paid in tithe were individually small, but in total large, their collection and assessment difficult, and the money often went to support a distant pluralist or a wealthy ecclesiastical corporation, such as a monastery, rather than to the local priest (**64**). Tithe had been attacked by Wyclif and the Lollards, and a Statute of 1536 referred to increasing attempts at evasion. Not only did the Church exact tithe, but it also enforced payment through its own courts. In London this was challenged and, in 1546, city tithe business was transferred from the church courts to the mayor's court (**120**). Tithe was a constant source of friction between layman and cleric, but it was the refusal to pay a different fee, a burial or mortuary fee, which began the case most damaging to the reputation of the church courts at this time. In 1511 a London merchant, Richard Hunne, refused to pay the fee for his son's burial, was eventually charged with heresy and committed to prison where, on 4 December 1514, he was found hanged in his cell. A murder verdict was declared, but the officers of the church courts were able to plead 'benefit of clergy' and thus escape the penalty of the common law (**42**). This situation created great outrage against the courts as benefit of clergy was being extended to all sorts of people only loosely connected with the Church; of seventy-six pleas of benefit of clergy made at York between 1452 and 1530, only thirteen involved priests or deacons (**62**).

Hunne's case was very damaging to the reputation of the courts, and a system in which the Church could appear as both judge and prosecution in cases involving its financial rights was under increasing attack from the common lawyers. Nevertheless it is important to stress that the Church did not always dispense justice so unfairly and that its courts offered a local and relatively cheap way of settling disputes in a wide area of moral and property law (**64, 89,** Lander).

The economic and legal powers of the Church meant that it was deeply involved in worldly affairs on its own behalf, and on behalf of others. Wolsey as Lord Chancellor stood at the apex of a long tradition of senior clerics in the service of the Crown, but even middle-ranking state servants like Richard Pace, Ambassador in Italy in the 1520s, were rewarded with church livings. In addition to the deaneries of St Paul and Exeter, Pace also received the arch-deaconry of Dorset and the rectory of Bangor for his services (**112**). The nobility followed the example of the Crown so that Richard Warde, steward to Lord Hussey and his estate manager, also held three parochial livings which had to be served by curates (**62**). Within the Church itself the management of its vast properties consumed much energy, and a man like Prior William More of Worcester, a good and capable administrator and a generous lord, appeared to have as much of the squire in him as of the monk (**72**). It seemed to some that the best livings in the Church were taken by those whose responsibility it was to service the institution, while the men responsible for the daily round of pastoral care often had to content themselves with meagre incomes. This structural weakness, rather than the scandalous lives of a few errant clerics, was the real problem facing the Church.

It was not a new problem and much the same could be said of the fifteenth-century Church, but in the years following 1500 the Church existed in an increasingly critical environment. The criticisms of the humanists have already been noted, but other factors were at work. It is well to recall that Colet's sermon was not designed to examine the ills of the Church but to find an antidote for the growth of heresy.

Heretics and reformers

Considered in a European context, heresy made a relatively late arrival in England, emerging only in the later decades of the four-teenth century when it became associated with the name of John Wyclif. Wyclif had supporters in academic circles, but some of his teachings soon found a following outside tbe university. This was particularly true of London and some provincial towns; in the countryside its support was drawn from lesser landowners and peasantry who soon became known as Lollards, in recognition of the importance which they placed on reading and expounding the scriptures in English. That apart, their beliefs centred on chal-lenging the priestly monopoly over the sacramental life of the

Church and in questioning some of the doctrines concerning the sacraments. In particular many Lollards denied the doctrine of transubstantiation, by which the Eucharist was said to be the real presence of the body of Christ. Lollardy also sought a partial disendowment of the Church (**19, 109**).

There is no doubt that groups of Lollards survived into the sixteenth century and that their beliefs foreshadowed some of the teachings of the reformers (**91, 129**). It is also clear that, from the late fifteenth century, the church authorities were becoming increasingly sensitive to heresy, but the precise relationship between Lollardy and the Reformation remains a matter for debate. To some scholars the Lollards appear as a living, coherent movement having something of a revival and providing a ready reception for the views of the reformers [**doc. 2**] (**42**). To others they appear as a fragmentary and highly localised survival which left large parts of the country unaffected, an irritation to the church authorities but, in themselves, not a major threat at national level (**109**). To some extent these differing views reflect differences in the regional distribution of Lollardy. In East Anglia, where seven heretics were burnt and a further eighteen brought to trial between 1499 and 1530, the spread of Protestantism was helped by the presence of small groups of Lollards, and the same is probably true of the Cotswolds (**129, 135**). Evidence from London and Kent would also support such an analysis and in another stronghold, the Chilterns, a vigorous tradition of heresy was kept alive in close proximity to Oxford University (**41**). Elsewhere, however, the evidence is very sketchy. Lollardy seems to have made little impact in the south-west, in Lancashire, or in Yorkshire, where such heretical views as did exist were found among individuals who had trade connections with either East Anglia or Europe (**55, 43**).

Over and above these regional differences it is possible to draw some general conclusions. The loose organisation and generally low social status of the Lollard groups did not make them in themselves the springboard for reform, but their scriptural piety and their criticism of the higher clergy placed them in a wider tradition about which the church authorities were very sensitive. With demands for spiritual renewal and reform coming from humanist clergy and others, the church authorities felt themselves to be under attack. In such a situation bishops and their officials were only too ready to see all criticism as heresy – as in the case of Richard Hunne. Thus they overreacted, and in their relentless pursuit of critics the church authorities determined to stamp out heresy. Often their actions in this regard, although instilling fear, merely served to harden anti-clerical attitudes. In such a climate, if the dissenting piety of the Lollards ever became associated with an intellectual movement critical of the Church, the authorities would indeed face a serious challenge. This is what came about when Lutheran ideas began to enter England early in the 1520s. It is too much to say that the Lollards were the spiritual ancestors of the reformers. They were, however, a small but significant part of the spiritual environment in which Protestantism was able to take root.

The earliest evidence we have for the arrival of Lutheran ideas in England relates to the circulation of books. An Oxford book-seller recorded the sale of twelve books by Luther in his ledger for 1520 and at the end of that year a public burning of Lutheran books was held in Cambridge (**42**). It was at Cambridge that the earliest identifiable English Protestants were to emerge in the 1520s as members of an informal group meeting at the White Horse Inn in the parish of St Edward. The customary leader of this group was Robert Barnes, Prior of the Augustinian Canons in the city. Its meetings coincided with the Cambridge careers of many of the major names of early English Protestantism: William Tyndale, Miles Coverdale, Thomas Bilney, John Frith, Hugh Latimer, and Thomas Cranmer, among others. The doctrine which really trans-formed their ideas and set Protestantism apart from all earlier heresies was Luther's notion of Justification by Faith, which was based on his study of St Paul's Epistle to the Romans and which he published in 1522. This doctrine, often misunderstood by the conservative theologians, placed the crucifixion as the central and sufficient act of salvation for all who had faith in it and acted in accordance with that faith. It was taken up and expounded most cogently for an English audience by William Tyndale in his English New Testament published abroad in 1525 and in his subsequent controversy with Sir Thomas More [**doc. 4**]. The importance of the doctrine was that it cut through and rendered theologically superfluous much of the intercessory and penitential ritual of the late medieval Church, of which indulgences were the most notorious object of abuse [**doc. 5**]. In harness with his doctrine, and given new life by it, more traditional themes emerged, such as the demand for the Bible in the vernacular language [**doc. 11**] and a rejection of the doctrine of transubstan-tiation. Some of the English reformers went further than Luther on this last matter and followed the teaching of the Swiss reformer Ulrich Zwingli, who saw the Eucharist simply as a memorial of the Last Supper and denied any real presence in the sacrament (**31, 98**).

This group of priests and students did not get a welcome reception from the authorities in Church or State, and many men were forced to flee to the Continent, from where they published books for their English followers which were distributed through merchant friends and sympathisers in the capital and other provincial centres. Some were to return to England in the 1530s only to die at the stake as heretics, but a few, such as Thomas Cranmer and Matthew Parker, were able to hold fast to their beliefs and ultimately to secure positions from which they could steer the course of the Church. That was all for the future: in the 1520s their position remained precarious and their influence beyond Cambridge University fragmentary (**31**). Certainly in London there were rumblings of debate, and in East Anglia awareness of the new ideas had come to merchants and men living by the sea, according to Bishop Nykke of Norwich, writing in 1530 (**41, 129**). The new ideas may also have influenced, and certainly drew attention to, the views of other provincial heretics such as Gilbert Johnson, a Dutchman living in York in 1528 (**43**). It is also likely that the White Horse Inn group influenced contemporaries at Cambridge, such as the Norfolk vicar Robert Buttelar who was in possession of Lutheran books in 1521. In two other east coast dioceses, Ely and Lincoln, a few priests came under suspicion and, between 1527 and 1532, were required to take an oath not to spread Lutheran views (**129, 25**). By 1530 the leading reformers had disciples in the provinces, particularly on the eastern seaboard, but their number was extremely small and their influence very localised. Protestantism at this date was unlikely to receive favour from a court headed by a King who had recently been honoured with the title Defender of the Faith and who was in the middle of delicate negotiations with the Papacy.

The presence of a native heretical tradition and the ultimate success of their cause must not blind us to the realities of the position in 1530; the early Protestant leaders were academic pioneers, often forced into exile, but with a small following among the clergy and laity at home. They were almost totally devoid of influence in the councils of the great, and steadfastness in their beliefs was to result in the sacrifice of their lives by many of them during the next three decades.

Conventional piety

Piety and religious sincerity were not confined solely to heretics or critics of the Church and, despite its difficulties, the Church continued to command vigorous and widespread support. Recent work has suggested that in England, as elsewhere, there was a revival of lay piety and involvement with the sacramental and pastoral life of the Church (**142**). Even in a county as relatively backward as Yorkshire the fifteenth-century gentry showed a considerable and discriminating provision for the Church in their wills. They left money for their churches, for priests and for masses for the dead in entirely conventional but none the less sincere terms (**110**). Lower down the social scale the laity of the diocese of Lincoln could participate in a wide variety of parochial institutions in the early sixteenth century, and many men must have been closely involved in the daily life of the Church through membership of confraternities and religious guilds and in their capacity as parochial officers and trustees caring for the property and fabric of their churches and chapels (**25, 91**). At Coventry in the early sixteenth century, the elaborate cycle of ritual culminating in the Corpus Christi procession and the mystery plays, in which all the civic crafts took part, drew large crowds of onlookers and gave religious and mystical expression to the fundamental harmony of the community and the social order (**115**). Other large towns had similar festivals and even in small towns, like Ashburton in Devon, there was a range of guilds dedicated to various saints and providing income for chaplains to assist in pastoral work (**10**). In large scattered parishes like Halifax laymen continued to endow chapels and priests to serve outlying settlements like Illingworth, where the chapel was founded in 1526 and continued to receive small grants from local laymen into the 1540s (**43**). This activity suggests that many laymen still placed a high value on the traditional services of the Church and the grants they made did much to assist the financing of pastoral provision. Thus a man like Thomas Worral, who was from 1518 stipendiary curate in the parish of St Michael Spurriergate, York, could make a reasonable living by additional services such as maintaining a chantry, conducting funerals and obits (masses for the dead), and managing properties left to the parish by various laymen (**60**, Cross). All these additional sources of income were of relatively recent origin and came from the laity. Even in London, 'the storm centre of the Reformation', the inhabitants continued to leave substantial sums for masses for the dead and other traditional services until the 1540s [**doc. 13a**].

In comparison with the lay material, the evidence from the clergy concerning conventional piety is less conclusive. One way to measure the strength of the Church in this period is to look at the numbers who were attracted to the priestly vocation. We have already seen how poorly paid were the unbeneficed parish clergy, but this fact did not prevent a surplus of priests over parishes in the early sixteenth century. Evidence from the dioceses of Lincoln and Ely suggests that men were still coming forward for the priesthood in considerable numbers up to 1520 (**24**). In Kent there were just under two clergymen, excluding monks, for each church in the 1520s and 1530s, and similar figures survive for the diocese of Lincoln in 1526. From about that date, however, signs of a decline in the numbers of vocations appear. From about 1527 ordinations no longer kept pace with the vacancies available and the upheavals of the 1530s hastened this decline dramatically (**60**, Zell). Even so, there were still almost two priests for every parish in the Lincoln diocese in 1543, but at this date the numbers may have been inflated by the former monks who had been turned out of their monasteries at the Dissolution (**25, 11**). Although monastic vocations had declined dramatically in the early sixteenth century, there were approximately seven hundred ex-religious in the diocese of Lincoln in 1541 (**11**).

Enough has been said to indicate the extent and variety of conventional piety. Much of that piety stemmed from a desire of the laity to be involved in the daily life of the Church and was directed towards greater pastoral provision in the parishes. On this matter both traditionalists and reformers had something in common. Intent as the hierarchy was on maintaining the privileges of the Church and eradicating heresy, the bishops, with a few honourable exceptions, failed to appreciate fully the significance of this trend in traditional piety. With that failure, the traditional piety of the laity was unable to withstand the onslaught of the following decades and went into retreat. In many cases that concern for involvement in the daily life of the Church became transformed and, in the last decades of the sixteenth century, was reasserted by Puritan laymen.

Part Two: Analysis

2 Institutional Reform

The difficulties of the Church and the apparent unwillingness of its leadership to undertake major reform had led to a stalemate in ecclesiastical affairs. Some bishops, such as John Fisher at Rochester and Robert Shereburne at Chichester, had indeed begun the process of reforming diocesan institutions but the work proceeded slowly and, as things turned out, was overtaken by events (**89**, Lander). The King wanted a divorce but the Pope, influenced by the Emperor Charles V, was both unwilling and unable to grant Henry's wish. In the summer of 1529 it was becoming clear that Wolsey, who had been in control of most royal policy for a decade and more, had failed to secure this and the King determined to remove him (**97**). There was however no acceptable replacement, and in a confused and uncertain political situation Henry summoned Parliament on 9 August 1529. During the next seven years this body was to carry through the legislation that was to alter forever the constitutional and economic position of the Church of England. Nobody considered this a possibility in 1529 and the title 'Reformation Parliament' was not coined until the beginning of this century, but contemporaries were clear that one of its objects was to be the reform of abuses in the Church. Fabyan's *Chronicle* contains the laconic entry in 1529, 'Parliament for the enormities of the clergy', and there were precedents for Parliamentary action in this area. Indeed after the Parliament of 1504, Bishop Nykke of Norwich wrote to Warham of Canterbury that 'the laymen be more bolder against the church than ever they were' (**46**). Both Nykke and Warham were still in office when Parliament met in the autumn of 1529.

The work of the Reformation Parliament can be divided into three stages. Between 1529 and 1531 there was relatively little direction of affairs as Parliament turned its attention to the abuses in the Church, such as non-residence by the clergy and the exaction of excessive fees by officials of the church courts. Royal initiative became more apparent during 1531, particularly over the Pardon of the Clergy, whereby the clergy were made to pay large sums for their alleged transgressions of the Statute of Praemunire (see page 20). From 1532 until 1534, as the matter of the divorce became more urgent, government policy, often dictated by the dominant figure of Thomas Cromwell, was consistently directed to ensure the supremacy of the Crown, in fact and ultimately in law, over the affairs of the Church in England [**docs. 7, 8**]. Once that had come about, policy was turned towards the disendowment of the Church, a policy which began only when Parliament was dissolved (**74**). Thus the work of this Parliament had identified the issues which were to dominate the institutional, though not the doctrinal, history of the Church until the end of our period. They can be drawn under four heads:

1 the relationship between the Crown and the papacy;
2 the role of the Crown and of statute law within the Church itself;
3 the need for administrative reform in the Church; and
4 the endowments of the Church.

Of course each aspect cannot be viewed in isolation and all were ultimately to have doctrinal implications, but at this stage it is best to consider them separately and in turn. Before doing so, however, we must spend some time on what proved to be the catalyst for such extensive and, some would say, revolutionary changes in the relationship between Church and State – the royal divorce.

The divorce

When the young King Henry VIII married Catherine of Aragon six weeks after his accession, he brought to an end six years of negotiation which had begun on 25 June 1503 when Henry, then about twelve years old, and Catherine, seventeen years of age, were betrothed. This betrothal had only been possible by virtue of a papal dispensation, for Catherine was the widow of Henry's elder brother, Prince Arthur, who had died when only fifteen years old. The nature of the dispensation granted was determined more by the realities of diplomacy than by the facts of the matter, for Catherine's Spanish advisors demanded that a dispensation on the grounds of affinity, which assumed that the young Queen's earlier marriage had been consummated, be sued for. This was done in order to protect the financial rights of the widowed princess, though Catherine herself always maintained that her first, and brief, marriage had not been consummated, a claim which even Henry ultimately accepted as true (**102**). In its earlier years the marriage between Henry and Catherine appears to have been a happy one, with the piety and learning of the Queen complementing her husband's more bellicose orthodoxy in religious matters. There was one shadow over the union, however, and that was Catherine's inability, despite several pregnancies, to produce a male heir for Henry. As the Queen grew older and the likelihood of successful child-bearing receded, her younger husband became infatuated elsewhere and, from 1525, was increasingly convinced that his marriage was unlawful, and was determined to replace Catherine with the more youthful Anne Boleyn.

At first, of course, the King looked to the Pope for an annulment of the marriage, but he was over-optimistic both about the strength of his case in canon law (**102**) and about the willingness of Pope Clement VII to set aside the decision of a predecessor (**95**). In law Henry based his case on a reading of two verses from Leviticus which seemed to prohibit marriage to one's dead brother's wife, despite an apparently contradictory passage in Deuteronomy allowing this. The traditional teaching of the Church, and the greater part of contemporary legal opinion, did not share Henry's reading of these passages and his case at law was very weak indeed. This weakness required complicated diplomatic manoeuvres, made even more sensitive because of the influence of Catherine's uncle, the Emperor Charles V, at the papal court.

Negotiations then turned on the legality of the original dispensation. Unable to get a satisfactory decision at Rome, the King and Wolsey tried to get the case heard in England, using the legatine powers granted to Wolsey. Though they appeared to be successful in this, it is doubtful whether the Pope ever really intended to allow the case to be heard in England, and his envoy, Cardinal Campeggio, continually delayed matters. Catherine refused to recognise the court after her first appearance before it and, finally, her appeal to have the case referred back to Rome was accepted by the Pope. In August 1529, the Treaty of Cambrai between the French and Charles brought the Pope and Emperor closer together. Whatever faint hope remained, the exclusion of England from the main negotiations meant that the policy of Henry and Wolsey was in ruins (**102, 112**).

There seemed to be no way forward. Attempts were made to sound out legal opinions at the great European universities in 1530, but it slowly emerged that little could be done in canon law. Where canon law could not act, statute law might provide the solution. Not only did this approach appeal to common lawyers and reflect a persistent theme among some humanist writers; it also found in Thomas Cromwell a policy-maker with the political acumen to see it through. Thus the process began of severing the constitutional link between the English Church and Rome, and of establishing the primacy of statute law within the realm. Though the first steps were hesitant, events moved swiftly in regard to the divorce, and final sentence was promulgated on 23 May 1533 by a new archbishop, Thomas Cranmer, at the head of a tribunal which had been approved by Parliament [**doc. 6**]. It would not be long before the rupture between Henry and the papacy was complete. Catherine was to die in January 1536 and Anne Boleyn was executed the following May, but their removal from the scene could not undo the work of the previous seven years.

Crown and papacy

Prior to the divorce, relations between the Crown and the papacy were dominated by three concerns: the need for the papacy to serve the Tudor dynasty; the desire of the Crown to control appointments to bishoprics; and the wish of Henry VIII to play a part in European diplomacy.

Support for the Tudors had been quickly granted by the papacy. On 27 March 1486 Pope Innocent VIII issued a bull excommunicating anyone challenging Henry VII's claims, and in addition refused 'benefit of clergy' to those clerics involved in opposition. Restrictions were also placed on the right of sanctuary which could be claimed. Thus by 1500 the papacy had not only given its support to the Tudors but had also been willing to restrict some of the privileges of the Church in order to assist the Crown in keeping the peace.

The second issue also involved the security of the realm, for a number of bishops had Yorkist sympathies. Using precedents from fourteenth-century legislation designed to secure the appointment of royal nominees to bishoprics, Henry VII went further and introduced the novel position of Cardinal Protector, based at the papal court and serving as a direct means of communication between King and Pope. From 1492 successive holders of this office ensured that royal nominees were duly appointed (**112**), a factor which proved important in the crisis of the 1530s when only one bishop, John Fisher of Rochester, stood out against the royal supremacy (**102**).

Good relations with the papacy were central to Henry VIII's

early ambitions to make a mark in European affairs. Some success was achieved with the Treaty of London of 1518; and Henry's attack on Luther, published in 1521 as the *Assertio Septem Sacramentorum*, gained him a papal title, 'Defender of the Faith' (*Fidei Defensor*). During the later 1520s, however, the divorce and the dominance of Catherine's uncle, the Emperor Charles V, over European affairs, destroyed Henry's plans. Though diplomatic activity continued, it became clear that the divorce could only be achieved by denying papal authority in England (**95, 102**).

This policy probably began late in 1530, but serious proposals only emerged in the following year when the Act of Praemunire was revived against the clergy who, in return for pardon, had to accept Henry as 'only supreme head of the English Church', though they did secure the addition of the qualifying phrase 'as far as the law of Christ allows' (**6**). The Submission of the Clergy in May 1532 marked a turning point, placing canon law beneath the law of the land [**doc. 7**], and leading to the resignation of Thomas More as Chancellor (**28**). The tenuous link with the papacy was effectively broken in March 1533 when the Act in Restraint of Appeals declared that the English Church was 'sufficient and meet of itself' to pronounce on the divorce. A papal Bull of Excommunication against Henry was threatened but not promulgated until 1538, by which time both Catherine and Anne Boleyn were dead (**49**).

Anglo-papal relations were of little importance thereafter until the accession of Mary in 1553. She sought to return England to full communion with Rome, but her advisors had come to terms with many features of the Henrician settlement and were cautious of her plans [**doc. 18**]. Her Spanish marriage increased those doubts (**78**), and the role of Cardinal Pole, the new Papal Legate, did little to dispel them. He had been absent from England since 1532, and was completely out of touch with English affairs, whilst his role in the Council of Trent had cast doubts on his own orthodoxy (**49**). Thus by the end of her reign, Mary had failed to gain the confidence of either the papacy or the English governing classes, and her policy was in some disarray (**78**). The accession of Elizabeth ushered in a fresh attempt at negotiations, but the experiments begun in the 1530s were not to be set aside again.

Crown and Parliament in the English Church

Renaissance scholarship was noted, amongst other things, for reviving debate over the rights and responsibilities of both governor and governed, and both churchmen and lawyers had exercised their minds on such matters. The medieval concept of society as an organic whole remained, but increasing attention was given to the role of the prince, or governor, in maintaining the unity and peace of society and the well-being of its members. Thus in 1509–1510 Edmund Dudley, in his book *The Tree of Commonwealth*, commanded the prince 'to maintain and support as far as in him lieth, the commonwealth of his subjects' (**86**). This doctrine had been expounded in the fourteenth century by Marsiglio of Padua and was revived in England by the jurist Christopher St German, conservative in religion and already in his sixties when he published a Latin Dialogue in 1523 on the laws of England and their relationship to more general theories of law and equity. St German was hardly a radical, yet in his book, and in the subsequent English version, he was careful to distinguish divine law from the law of the Church, and he placed temporal matters firmly within the control of the state, making it clear that it was the King in Parliament (or under the law of the land) and not the King himself who was supreme in such matters. In sum, his work did not challenge the existence of papal and church courts, but it restricted their competence to a much narrower range of strictly spiritual matters. Of course his view was a minority one and not shared by lawyers like Sir Thomas More. The point however is that these matters, touching the nature of sovereignty and the relations between Church and State, were under discussion in learned legal quarters in the early days of the Reformation Parliament and even before (**48, 54**).

Hardly any of those MPs who arrived at Westminster in November 1529 were aware of this debate, and none foresaw its outcome. Their more immediate concerns were with the abuses in the Church. The attitude of MPs may have been expressed in a draft bill submitted by the Commons and subsequently modified, probably by Thomas Cromwell. In this draft the judges of the church courts were described as 'a sort of ravenous woolvys nothing alles attending but there onelie pryvate lucres and satisfaction of the covetous and insaisable appetites of the said prelatis and ordynaries' (**74**). This was a clear echo of the tone adopted by Simon Fish [**doc. 3**]. The legislation that passed in this first session of 1529 was directed against abuses: acts regulating the fees payable for mortuary and for probate (the proving of wills) and for defining the conditions under which clerics could be pluralists became law. The clergy in the House of Lords attempted to block the passage of these bills, but were unsuccessful. Once they had been passed, about two hundred prosecutions were brought against clergy infringing these statutes. This sort of legislation was of a traditional sort and did not break new ground, though the fierceness of anti-clerical attitudes among MPs was marked. There were, however, some signposts to the future, though we must be careful not to read too much into them in these uncertain early stages of policy. In Convocation there was a vague rumour circulating about a proposed reform and appropriation of some monastic property (**74**). This rumour was extremely hazy about the nature of the proposals, but ideas along such lines had been in circulation before that date and Wolsey himself had suppressed thirty monastic houses between 1525 and 1528 (**72**). At the end of its first session Parliament had set about the reform of church abuses in a vigorous but essentially traditional manner. The King had no intention of permitting the assembly to initiate policy, nor was it allowed to discuss the divorce. In Henry's eyes Parliament had not yet become the ally and instrument of royal policy, and the uncertainty of that policy meant that the next meeting of Parliament did not take place until the beginning of 1531. During the interval in 1530 the negotiations over the divorce were deteriorating, and Thomas Cromwell began to emerge as an influential advisor on royal policy, becoming a member of the Council by the end of that year (**74**).

Cromwell's arrival was ultimately to give more consistent direction to royal policy, but this did not happen overnight and uncertainty was to continue for at least another year or two. Nevertheless the subsequent history of the legislative programme cannot be understood without some consideration of the ideas upon which it was based. The theoretical framework for Cromwell's policy is difficult to disentangle, for he was essentially a practical man. Pragmatism, or the art of achieving the possible, is in itself a legitimate political stance to adopt, but it would be unfair to suggest that Cromwell stopped there. The other clue to his views lies in his legal training and in his respect for the law and, in particular, for statute law. It is in this respect for secular law that Cromwell differed from that other great respecter of law, his political opponent, Sir Thomas More. Where More was inclined to view law in an essentially theological sense and as a restraint upon the inherent sinfulness of man, Cromwell saw the role of the law from the standpoint of practical philosophy as an aid to the 'common weal'. He did not himself write any theoretical works, and his views are enshrined best in the legislation that he prompted, and particularly in the preambles to statutes. He did, however, promote theoretical works by others (**48, 54**).

Two of these were published in 1535: Thomas Starkey's *Exhortation to the people instructing theym to Virtue and Obedience* and William Marshall's translation of the *Defensor Pacis* of Marsiglio of Padua, first written in 1324. Starkey's book has been described as the first expression of the *via media*, or middle way, in English religious and political life. His notion that there were 'things indifferent' (*adiaphora*) which men could not be compelled to believe and which were, therefore, not to be enforced by law was to become an important theme in the religious disputes of Elizabeth's reign. Marshall's translation of Marsiglio attempted to place the ideas of the fourteenth-century Italian firmly in the English context. Thus when Marsiglio made reference to law-making by the 'commune' or assembled population of the Italian city-state, Marshall was careful to gloss this with notes such as 'in all this long tale he speaketh not of the rascall multitude, but of the parlyamente'. Statute law was therefore the foundation and chief instrument of a sovereign royal power ruling over a unitary Church and State, but that law was restricted in its operation to matters essential to public order and well-being; it was not to pry into conscience over 'things indifferent'. However, it is unlikely that this last distinction was always observed in the hurly-burly of everyday politics; and it was in politics, the transference of theoretical ideas into practical policy, that Cromwell excelled (**48**).

The second session of Parliament occupied the early months of 1531 and marked a transitional stage in the development of policy. The central business, though not strictly parliamentary, concerned the charge of *praemunire* made against the whole clergy of the realm. The essence of the charge was that, in accepting Wolsey's legatine authority, the clergy had given support to an external jurisdiction within the King's realm. There was no intention of bringing the whole of the clergy before the courts. Indeed, the original plan to indict fifteen leading clerics in the courts was abandoned, and it appears that the accusation was merely a device to bring the question of papal jurisdiction into the open and to raise a substantial sum of money – £100,000 – from the clergy in return for a pardon. It is true that the 'supreme headship' was first formulated in the prologue to the charge; but, while this may represent royal acceptance of Cromwell's concept of caesaropapism (joining both spiritual and temporal power in the monarch), its implications were nullified by the clergy, who demanded that the phrase 'as far as the law of God allows' be inserted. It seems clear that, at this stage, Henry was satisfied with threatening the clergy and extorting money from them.

In Parliament itself the members began where they had left off in 1529, and a number of devices to reform the Church were in circulation. Of these, two deserve mention: one raised the question of translating the Bible into English in order to secure an orthodox rival to the proscribed text of Tyndale; the other proposed that the trial of heretics be transferred from the jurisdiction of the bishops to a 'standing council' appointed by the government (**74**). By the time Parliament met again at the beginning of 1532, affairs at court had moved decisively in favour of Thomas Cromwell.

Matters of religion were not discussed in the early weeks of the session, but in mid-February 1532 the Commons complained of the cruelty of the bishops in their proceedings against heretics. The members were no doubt concerned about the recent revival of heresy trials in which Sir Thomas More had been active [**doc. 4**], but whether their complaint was a spontaneous one or orchestrated by Cromwell is a matter of some dispute. Cromwell had already drawn up the Supplication against the Ordinaries but had to await the emergence of a consensus in the Commons and to ensure that the government, and especially the King, were not associated with such a radical document. The Supplication challenged the right of the clergy in Convocation to 'make divers fashions of laws and ordinances concerning temporal things; and some of them be repugnant to the laws and statutes of your realm; not having nor requiring your most royal assent of the same laws by them so made, nor any assent or knowledge of your lay subjects is had to the same' (**6**). This amounted to a demand that the legislative independence of the clergy in Convocation be cancelled. It was Cromwell's intention that this should be achieved by statute, but events, and Henry's own view of his prerogative, overtook his calculations. The Supplication was presented to the King on 18 March and he, apparently showing little interest, passed it on to the clergy in Convocation (**74**). Their reply, based on a draft of Stephen Gardiner, asserted the right of the Church to make its own law and was sent to the King on 27 April. The reply angered the King, perhaps because it challenged the theories of caesaropapism he had begun to espouse, and he responded quickly (**87**). In dismay the bishops offered no leadership, but on 8 May the lower clergy countered by asking Henry to defend the traditional liberties of the Church. This was a disastrous move and two days later Henry demanded a submission from the clergy to the effect that Convocation could make no church law, past, present or future, that was contrary to the law of the land and which did not have the royal assent. This submission was made unwillingly by the clergy on 16 May, two days after Parliament had been prorogued. It amounted to a complete capitulation by the Church and an acknowledgement of the legislative supremacy of the Crown in everything except matters of doctrine (**130**).

Parliament had also passed the Act in Conditional Restraint of Annates. This removed the right of the Pope to tax the clergy and ensured that patronage rested with the King. This attack on the privileges of the Pope was followed through in 1533 with the passing of the Act in Restraint of Appeals which, though directed to the ordering of Anglo-papal relations, included in its preamble the first and most famous declaration of the claims for royal authority in the Church. The preamble began,

> 'Where by divers sundry old authentic histories and chronicles it is manifestly declared and expressed that this realm of England is an empire, and so hath been accepted in the world, governed by one supreme head and king having the dignity and royal estate of the imperial crown of the same, unto whom a body politic, compact of all sorts and degrees of people divided in terms and by names of spirituality and temporality, be bounden and owe to bear next to God a natural and humble obedience . . .' (**6**)

English kings had long claimed that their crown was an imperial one. What was new in the preamble was the concept of the nation as an 'empire', for on this statement rested the claim for independent national sovereignty. Within that empire the Crown was supreme in Church and State, but the reference to both 'spirituality and temporality', suggested that clergy and laity continued to have independent jurisdiction under the Crown. In this way the supremacy of the Crown was clearly stated, but the practical implications still needed definition. Though that supremacy was embodied in statute, the precise role of statute and of Parliament in the Church remained unclear.

The royal supremacy was worked out more fully in the legislation of 1534. The Act in Restraint of Annates confirmed the legislation of 1532. The right to grant dispensations from canon law was transferred from the Pope to the Archbishop of Canterbury, whose authority in this respect was nevertheless subject to appeal to the Lord Chancellor. Parliament also removed the annual tax of 1*d.* per household traditionally paid by the English Church to Rome. Cromwell's earlier intention to have the Submission of the Clergy endorsed by statute was also achieved [**doc. 7**] during the spring session which ended with an Act of Succession, establishing the succession to the throne in the heirs of Henry and Anne Boleyn (**6, 74**).

In the autumn of 1534 the Act of Supremacy was passed. This not only confirmed the supreme headship of the Crown, which the earlier statutes had expressed, but also gave the King specific powers within the Church. Henry was not merely the secular head and protector of the clergy, but he also annexed the power of visitation, the right to discipline the clergy and to correct the opinions of preachers, the supervision of canon law and of doctrine, and the right to try heretics [**doc. 8**]. Though he never claimed a priestly or sacerdotal function for himself, in matters of jurisdiction Henry acquired quasi-episcopal status by the granting of these powers (**47**). Nor was he slow to act. In 1535 Thomas Cromwell was appointed Vicegerent, or Vicar-general, and thus had wide-ranging powers within the Church. It was in this capacity that he conducted the visitation of the monasteries which served as a prelude to the dissolution of the smaller houses [**doc. 9**] (**114**).

The royal supremacy was thus established in its fullest caesaro-papist form. What still required definition was the precise role of Parliament in this supremacy. Statute law had carried the programme through, but Henry was careful to confine the role of Parliament to discussion of church affairs and to the fixing of penalties for those who transgressed the laws. The law of the Church could not contradict the law of Parliament but, though it required the royal assent, it did not yet require parliamentary approval. When Henry used the supremacy to define doctrine in the Act of Six Articles (1539) he was careful to restrict the role of Parliament to fixing penalties (**6**). Earlier attempts to formulate doctrine were carried through by Convocation, acting directly on the wishes of the King.

During the reign of Henry VIII the royal supremacy meant exactly that and no more, but the accession of a minor changed the balance of the relationship between the King and Parliament on this issue. The establishment of Protestantism under Edward VI was carried through by statute, and the Acts of Uniformity went a long way to claiming that the liturgy of the Church and, by implication, the doctrine that liturgy expressed were based on the authority of Parliament. Thus the royal supremacy came to be exercised by the King in Parliament, rather than by the King in his own right (**69, 70**). When Mary wished to return the nation to communion with Rome, she could only bring this about through Parliament, which alone had the authority to remove previous statutory legislation. Thus at the accession of Elizabeth the essentially personal supremacy of Henry VIII had acquired a new dimension, involving Parliament not only in matters of jurisdiction but also in matters of doctrine. When Mary wished to surrender her own powers as the Supreme Head of the Church, she could only do so with the co-operation of Parliament. From being an instrument of the supremacy, Parliament had become a partner in it (**39**).

Administrative reforms

Much of the early legislation of the Reformation Parliament, culminating in the Supplication against the Ordinaries, was directed against those abuses in the Church mentioned in Chapter 1. It would be wrong, however, to suggest that the Church was doing nothing to correct matters, and there is some irony in the fact that, as Parliament was sitting, Convocation was busy looking at the same problems. Recent studies suggest that, in the first half of Henry VIII's reign, a number of dioceses were in the hands of outstanding administrators who were both conscientious and competent. A surviving court book of one of these, William Attwater, Bishop of Lincoln, shows the range of work being done by a conscientious bishop in the years between 1514 and 1520. In a large diocese covering seven counties Bishop Attwater was constantly on the move between April and September, ordaining clergy, conducting visitations, and correcting offences of both clergy and laity. He conducted matters in person on over half of the occasions on which his court sat, and its judgements were fair. The business was carried out in a painstaking and detailed manner and the evidence from Lincoln shows that the charges made in the Commons' Supplication were greatly exaggerated. The cases brought in Attwater's court were not frivolous and the fees charged were not extortionate. Thus, on the eve of the break with Rome, a large part of England was subject to regular personal visitation and correction by its bishop (**25**). A similar story emerges from the diocese of Chichester, where the evidence suggests that the events of the 1530s, instead of reforming, had a 'direct and dismal effect upon the exercise of ecclesiastical jurisdiction' (**89**, Lander). Parliamentary and royal attacks on the Church left the bishops demoralised, and royal injunctions and visitations in 1535 posed a further threat to their authority. The result was that the church courts suffered a serious loss of esteem. From the 1530s there followed a steady but inexorable decline in respect for sentences of excommunication and an increasing tendency for defendants to absent themselves from the court when charged. By the end of our period the amount of business before the courts had increased again, but many cases were not followed through to judgement. The character of the work in the courts changed also. Their jurisdiction over matters touching morality and reputation remained intact, but in matters concerning property, such as tithe and probate, the courts suffered some small encroachment from the common law [**doc. 27**] (**64**).

Discipline, however, was only one aspect of episcopal responsibility. A bishop was also a pastor, the father of his flock. There were some early sixteenth-century bishops, like John Fisher,*who placed a very high priority on their pastoral responsibilities, particularly on preaching. The events of the 1530s, however, deprived the Church of Fisher's leadership, and conservative bishops, largely out of sympathy with the drift of religious policy, provided few pastoral initiatives in the reign of Henry VIII. A few reformers, such as Shaxton of Chichester in 1538, used their office to further the Reformation (**42**), but most of these resigned or were forced to lie low after the conservative Act of Six Articles in 1539 (**138**). Only in the reign of Edward VI did the reformers come into their own, and one, John Hooper, Bishop of Worcester and Gloucester, demonstrated particularly well the pastoral emphasis on regular preaching and instruction for the laity. He also arranged for the less well qualified parish clergy to follow a regular course of scriptural study and, like Bishop William Attwater, travelled extensively throughout his dioceses [**doc. 17**] (**137**). Others, such as Miles Coverdale at Exeter, followed suit, but their time was limited and, at the accession of Mary, much still remained to be done (**76**).

Nor was the Marian Church unaware of its pastoral responsibilities. The bishops were appointed for their loyalty to Rome, but they were also learned men. In 1555 they were required to reside within their bishoprics, to adopt a more simple lifestyle, to preach regularly and to examine more carefully the knowledge and learning of candidates for the priesthood (**78**). Again, however, their efforts were curtailed by time and, at the accession of Elizabeth, they all resigned.

The events of the 1530s had therefore both a negative and a positive consequence for church administration. The decline in status and respect which the church courts suffered made the task of enforcing church law and religious uniformity more difficult for the bishops. On the other hand, the bishops themselves were much more concerned for their pastoral obligations, resided in their dioceses, and were less involved in secular activities. By 1560 they were also, by and large, less well off than their predecessors had been in 1520.

The endowments of the Church

Although the early years of Henry VIII's reign had witnessed an increase in royal taxation of the Church, the issue had not provoked any serious opposition from the clergy in the years prior to 1530. Indeed with the Conditional Restraint of Annates in 1532 it looked as if the Crown might well be relieving the English Church of some of the customary dues paid to the papacy. However, the sums of money demanded from Convocation in return for pardon from *praemunire* may have served as a warning to the clergy that the Crown was unlikely to ignore the wealth of the Church when it needed to look for increased income. In 1534 not only were annates, which represented the first year's profit from bishoprics, transferred to the Crown, but a similar payment, now known as First Fruits, was demanded from all ecclesiastical livings of whatever value. In addition the Act provided for an annual levy by the Crown of one-tenth of the profit of church livings, and the Church itself, through the bishops, was made responsible for the administration, collection and payment of these new taxes. The Act also arranged for the appointment of commissioners to survey all the church livings, so that these taxes could be assessed on an up-to-date and realistic valuation of clerical income. This great and detailed survey, known as the *Valor Ecclesiasticus*, was compiled in 1535 with taxation in mind and has come down to historians as the starting point for our knowledge of the wealth of the Church during the Reformation. It is vivid testimony to the administrative thoroughness of Thomas Cromwell (**89**, Heal). The Act of First Fruits and Tenths, therefore, was an attempt to ensure regular and realistic taxation of the Church, but even more radical ideas were in circulation in 1534. A document was prepared proposing the wholesale nationalisation of Church land and wealth, which would have reduced the status of bishops and clergy to that of being the paid servants of the Crown (**48**). Such a measure was too radical, but in 1536 legislation was passed which set on foot a process which resulted in the transfer, over the next sixty years, of about 25 per cent of the total land in England from the Church to the laity [**doc. 9b**] (**114**).

Though there had been much humanist criticism of monastic life in the early sixteenth century, the influence of these critics in England did not extend beyond the universities and court circles before the 1530s. The monasteries and friaries were spread unevenly throughout England: only fourteen were in Lancashire, but Lincolnshire contained sixty-six religious houses in 1535. As is likely with such diversity, standards varied greatly. At Carishead in north Lancashire the prior in the 1530s was suspected of murder (**55**), but at Evesham in Worcestershire the monks appear to have maintained an intellectual and spiritual life which also involved nearby houses (**72**). Between these extremes, however, most monasteries shared the characteristics of the Lancashire houses which, though not disreputable, had declined in moral authority as a result of over-involvement in local secular affairs (**55**).

In 1535, when the process of disendowment was initiated, there were no real precedents for such policy. The Swiss example was tainted with heresy and therefore unacceptable to a doctrinally orthodox regime, and few people in England would have been aware of the activities of the King of Sweden in turning over some important monastic wealth to the State (**114**). In England, the dissolution of the lesser monasteries was a careful and thorough policy, largely orchestrated by Thomas Cromwell [**doc. 9a**]. Few of these smaller monasteries were able to sustain a vigorous monastic community, numbers were small and recruitment falling (**114**), but the monasteries still had their defenders. The suppression of the houses in Lincolnshire and the North brought forth a series of localised rebellions known collectively as the Pilgrimage of Grace. The motives of the rebels were mixed and there is no doubt that the very thoroughness of royal policy was an important factor. The defence of the monasteries became the rallying call for rebels in many areas of the north and, though the risings owed much to social and economic grievances, it is hard to deny the potent force of religion in sustaining the rebellions (**51**). It was a point not lost on Cromwell, and the process by which the lesser monasteries came into the hands of the Crown over the next two years was carefully managed. The rights of local landholders who had leases from the monasteries were recognised, and for many of them the dissolution meant no more than a change in landlord. Many of them were brought into the dissolution itself, acting as surveyors or bailiffs on behalf of the Crown, the new owner (**114**).

At the end of 1537 the great and wealthy priory of Lewes was induced to surrender to the Crown and, from that date, it became clear that government policy was directed to the dissolution of the greater as well as of the lesser monasteries (**72**). Following the surrender of Lewes, the dissolution of the larger houses took place, not by Act of Parliament, but in a series of private agreements, albeit ones forced by circumstance, between monastic heads and royal commissioners (**114**). A few men, notably the Abbots of Colchester, Reading and Glastonbury, stood out against the policy, refused to hand over their lands, and were executed for treason, but on the whole the suppression of these houses went ahead remarkably peacefully (**72**). An Act of 1539 confirmed the rights of the Crown as the legal owner of those lands surrendered or to be surrendered, and by 1540 the process was more or less complete. The Crown had acquired substantial new estates, a great number of landholders found themselves with a new landlord (**114**), and many ex-monks and nuns had to adjust to a new life, either within or outside the Church (**11**).

The Crown needed the machinery to administer its new-found wealth, and established in 1536 the Court of Augmentations specifically for this purpose (**100**). The Crown never really intended to retain all the former monastic lands in its own hands and had always envisaged selling off part of these properties. During Henry's reign at least, though some crown officials received grants of land [**doc. 9b**], the Crown did not squander this property by disposing of it cheaply. On the whole the lands were sold for a reasonable price, and by 1547 about £800,000 had been raised in this way (**114**).

That the Crown was able to find purchasers for the lands does itself call for explanation. Who were the purchasers? It has already been suggested that laymen as lessees had a substantial interest in monastic property before the dissolution. Such men, traditionally associated with monastic estates, were often the ultimate purchasers of their leasehold lands. Others to take advantage were local landowners, often of gentry status, who wished to consolidate their estates, and in this way the sale of monastic land reinforced the local social structure. Very few new men or outsiders exploited the market and there was no wholesale revolution in the pattern of landownership among the laity. For the poor, and the customary tenants, the change in land ownership does not seem to have resulted in a loss of their customary rights or in more rapacious exploitation by their new landlords (**114, 83**).

For the monks and nuns turned out of their communities the break with tradition was more sudden and, in the short term, disruptive. No doubt, the 'voluntary' surrenders of many of the larger monasteries were made easier by the relatively generous terms offered to the more important inmates, such as the Abbot of Romsey who received £266 a year. At Buckfast Abbey in 1539 some £177 out of a total of almost £500 a year received was set aside for pensions for the inmates, and in 1558 the Crown was still paying out over 40 per cent of the remaining profits of the monastery as pensions. But any policy which removed the livelihood of 9,000 men and women was bound to lead to some hardship, and the majority of pensions provided for subsistence at best. The nuns fared worst of all, but many ex-monks were able to find their way into the ranks of the parochial or chantry clergy (**11, 21**). However, such relief as was offered by alternative employment in the chantries was short-lived, for in 1547 these institutions were also dissolved by Act of Parliament (**73**).

During the 1540s Henry VIII set about a series of exchanges with a number of bishops whereby they were granted rectory estates in return for handing over manors and other lands to the Crown. The policy continued under Edward VI and by 1553 the annual income of all the bishops in England and Wales amounted to £22,500 a year, a drop of £7,000 a year since 1535 (**61**). This attack on episcopal estates was reversed in the reign of Mary when many bishops had land restored to them, so that by 1558 their joint income had recovered to just over £1,000 below the 1525 figure (**61, 76**, Pogson).

Much of the criticism of monasteries was based on the belief that their wealth could be used more positively for the common good, and in particular for educational purposes. This transfer of resources did not take place. Some of the former monastic property was used to establish new bishoprics out of large dioceses; thus Peterborough and Oxford were created from Lincoln, and Chester from York and Lichfield. But their endowment was meagre and this made administration difficult (**89**, Haigh, Sheils). Direct educational endowment was minimal, Trinity College, Cambridge and the refounding of Wolsey's college at Oxford, renamed Christchurch, being the sum total (**114**). After the dissolution of the chantries in 1547, many of their schools were refounded and placed on a more secure economic base, but the growth in educational provision in Tudor England was chiefly the result of private benefactors rather than of Crown policy (**90**). Sizeable though it was, this growth was piecemeal and haphazard, and was not the sort of programme envisaged by the humanist reformers of the 1530s (**71**).

3   Doctrinal Changes

When Henry VIII assumed the title of Supreme Head of the Church in England in the 1530s, only one of his bishops, John Fisher, refused to acknowledge his claim. Others such as Cuthbert Tunstall of Durham had misgivings, but even a staunch conservative like Stephen Gardiner of Winchester could write a tract, *De Vera Obedientia*, in defence of the royal title (**102, 87**). But when in 1559 the first Elizabethan Parliament passed the Act of Supremacy, which gave the Queen the more restricted title of Supreme Governor, the whole of the episcopal bench, including the aged Tunstall, resigned (**67, 131**). The difference in the two responses lay not in the titles themselves, but in their doctrinal implications. Henry's claims in the 1530s chiefly concerned matters of jurisdiction and of canon law, and there was no anticipation of a departure from traditional doctrinal orthodoxy. The Elizabethan Act was accompanied by an Act of Uniformity which, for all its qualifications, established a religion undoubtedly Protestant. In this chapter we will consider this change in doctrinal allegiance in so far as it was apparent among the political and intellectual leaders of the nation.

Protestants and reformers in the 1530s

The 1530s began inauspiciously for Protestants. Some of the early Cambridge Protestants had followed Tyndale into exile at Antwerp. From there they continued their work of translating the Bible, and they engaged in a pamphlet warfare with their intellectual and political opponents (**31**), chief among whom was Sir Thomas More. More, as Lord Chancellor, was partly responsible for the renewed attack on heresy in the years between 1529 and 1532 [**doc. 4**] (**54**). The most famous victim of this campaign was Thomas Bilney, burnt at the stake in Norwich in 1531. Bilney's views were difficult to define and there was no conclusive proof that they were unorthodox. He had been dismissed after an earlier trial in 1527 and was a popular figure in Norwich. In 1531, however, he ignored a prohibition on preaching without licence and was also charged with distributing Tyndale's books. The authorities proceeded against him as a relapsed heretic despite the uncertainty of the earlier charges, and his burning provoked strong local opposition. If his crime was the distribution of Protestant books, he was in company with other Protestants, mostly active in London, who also suffered at this time, and More himself was probably behind the royal proclamation of 22 June 1530 prohibiting the circulation of heretical books and Bible translations. This document suggests that the authorities were already concerned by the spread of heretical literature and also illustrates the difficulties under which the Protestants laboured at this time (**42, 129**). For most of its adherents, Protestantism was a calling fraught with personal danger. A few men – very few – associated with the early Protestants had attained minor positions in the Church and universities, but, at this date, the evidence for their Protestantism is not direct and does not come from knowledge of their own views. Such a man was Thomas Cranmer. His rapid rise to the Archbishopric of Canterbury was due to his role in the royal divorce and also to his friendship with the Boleyn family (**101**). The position of men like Cranmer improved greatly with the rise of the Boleyns and the emergence of Thomas Cromwell, and it was through the patronage of these people that the reformers first gained a hearing at court (**124**).

It may be too early to describe a reformer like Cranmer as a Protestant in 1534, for we have little evidence of his doctrinal position (**27**). Faced with the orthodoxy of Henry VIII, the court reformers had, in any case, to be circumspect and discreet: the more so as Protestant ideas, frequently spread by the underground dissemination of a wide variety of differing books, often emerged in a heterodox form. Fired with the enthusiasm of converts, many of the Protestants were not noted for their discretion. Thus we find that, during the 1530s, the constraints of politics often forced Cranmer and Cromwell to take action against men with whom they had some sympathy. There is no better illustration of this than the case of John Lambert, a convert of Bilney and a friend of Tyndale. He had been prosecuted for heresy and kept in custody until 1532. Thereafter he ran a school in London but, in 1536, fell foul of conservative opinion because of his attacks on the worship of the saints. Tried by three reforming bishops – Cranmer, Shaxton and Latimer – Lambert refused their offer of a compromise and was again imprisoned. By 1538 he was again free, but got involved in a disputation with other Lutherans about the doctrine of the Eucharist. His position was set down in a *Treatise upon the Sacrament* and represented a denial of transubstantiation. Ill-advisedly he had dedicated it to Henry VIII who himself appeared, clad in white from head to foot, at Lambert's trial. The trial ended in Lambert's conviction, and he was burnt as a heretic (**42**).

Lambert was a graduate, but many other leaders of local Protestant groups were not. Men like John Harridaunce, a London bricklayer, who expounded the scriptures to large audiences in his house and garden, were always likely to embarrass their more exalted sympathisers. [Protestantism in the 1530s was thus a diffuse and unstructured phenomenon with no chain of command.] Even the few sympathisers who attained bishoprics could exasperate policy-makers by their enthusiasm. Thus in 1538 Thomas Cromwell had to rebuke Nicholas Shaxton, Bishop of Salisbury, when the bishop attempted to replace a Catholic reader at Reading Abbey with a reformer. However the very appearance of Shaxton on the episcopal bench marked a significant advance for Protestantism, the more so as he was joined by the great preacher Hugh Latimer (**46**). Latimer's sermon before Convocation in 1536 makes a striking contrast to that of Colet twenty-five years before. Latimer inveighed against traditional religious practices in no uncertain terms, was critical of purgatory, of saints' days, of images and ceremonies and much else in conventional piety [**doc. 10**]. [Protestantism had clearly arrived in a position of authority, but it still represented a minority view. Its achievement at this time lay not in the establishing of a Church or in the control of policy, but in stressing the central importance of a scriptural foundation for religious activities.]

Its greatest success, therefore, was the translation of the Bible into English. In the eyes of the authorities biblical translation had a bad pedigree, being associated with the heretical Lollards and also with Lutheranism. In his translation of the New Testament in 1525 William Tyndale, in exile, incurred the wrath of the English authorities by his avowedly Protestant leanings. Key words were given Protestant renderings, such as 'congregation' and 'senior', rather than the traditional translations of 'church' and 'priest' respectively (**84**). Throughout the years 1525 to 1534 Tyndale had attracted a series of assistants and collaborators in his work, and two of them, Miles Coverdale and John Rogers, worked with him shortly before his martyrdom in 1536. In that same year the Convocation of Canterbury petitioned the King for an orthodox rival to Tyndale's translation, 'that the holy Scripture shall be translated into the vulgar tongue by certain upright and learned men, to be meted out and delivered to the people for their instruction' (**42**). In the following year Miles Coverdale published his translation of the complete Bible in Zurich, and it was soon published in England. The translation did not, as yet, receive whole-hearted support from the government, and Cranmer and Cromwell continued to proceed cautiously. Nevertheless in 1537 another translation of the Bible appeared; it was known as the Matthew Bible from the pseudonym of the translator John Rogers, and royal permission was granted for its sale throughout the realm. More importantly the royal injunctions of 1538 required that a copy be placed in every church, and the bishops were urged to encourage the laity to read the Bible. Eventually these individual efforts were organised by Cromwell, who entrusted Coverdale with the compilation of an offical translation. Despite the opposition of some conservative bishops the Great Bible appeared in 1539, to be followed in 1540 by a special cheap edition for private reading. The Bible of 1539 moderated some of Tyndale's more partisan terminology and even included notes referring to the Catholic Vulgate. There is no doubt that official support for the vernacular Bible represented a considerable success for the reformers, who had also achieved some other successes [**doc. 11**] (**42, 85**).

The Ten Articles were passed by Convocation at the wish of the King in 1536 and represent the first steps of the Supreme Head in the definition of doctrine. The Articles themselves were strictly orthodox in content except in two important features. The article concerned with the Eucharist was left ambiguous and open to orthodox or Lutheran interpretation but, more radically, the number of sacraments discussed was reduced from the customary seven to the three deemed necessary for salvation – baptism, penance and the Eucharist. These Articles were endorsed by Royal Injunctions promulgated in the same year, wherein the clergy were also exhorted to encourage moderation in traditional piety and to point out that acts of charity to the poor and others were just as praiseworthy and valuable for salvation. Thus these injunctions began to make clear the social gospel of the 'commonwealth group' in the context of religion. The attack on images and other traditional practices was taken further in the Injunctions of 1538, which also endorsed the English Bible and required the clergy to make more thorough examinations of the religious understanding of the laity (**9, 48**).

Between publication of the Injunctions of 1536 and those of 1538 a large committee of clergy compiled and published the *Institution of a Christian Man* in July 1537. This volume, usually called *The Bishops' Book*, indicated the delicate balance of forces that existed between conservatives and reformers among the episcopate (**117**). It restored those sacraments of matrimony, confirmation, holy orders and extreme unction which had been excluded from the Ten Articles and, all in all, seems to reflect the influence of the conservatives. Nevertheless it remained ambiguous on the enforcement of belief in transubstantiation and stressed the importance of Justification by Faith and of Scripture (**42**). Government policy in the latter half of the 1530s, therefore, gave some hope to Protestants, but the Mass remained as the central expression of the people's religion.

In 1530 the Protestants were confined to a few academic exiles with no friends at court. By 1539 they had a voice in the King's Council, a few representatives on the bench of bishops, and small groups of adherents among the clergy and laity. In addition they had more widespread support for their scriptural, if not their doctrinal, position and had produced works like Simon Fish's *Sum of Holy Scripture*, published in English in 1535, which were to influence later generations. As yet, however, they remained a small, if significant minority whose position was still precarious. The doctrinal orthodoxy of the King and the collapse of negotiations with the Lutheran princes proved to be the undoing of Thomas Cromwell in 1539. With his fall the balance of forces was once again tipped in favour of the conservatives (**47, 119**).

Conservative ascendancy 1539–1546

In the early summer of 1539 Henry VIII resolved upon settling religious disputes in the realm and called upon a committee of the House of Lords to establish 'a devise for the unity in the religion' (**47**). Under the chairmanship of Cromwell as Vicegerent, the committee was deliberately structured to create deadlock between the reformers and the Catholics and probably never met. Instead the King, acting through the Duke of Norfolk, presented six questions to the House of Lords on central issues in dispute between Catholics and reformers. The questions were so phrased as to demand traditional answers and the reformers could offer only token resistance. The ensuing Act of Six Articles was a total defeat for the reformers and brought the resignation of the Protestant bishops Latimer and Shaxton. Its clauses enforced belief in transubstantiation, under penalty of being burnt; denied the necessity of Communion in both kinds for the laity; required that priests remained celibate and that others under vows of chastity should not set those vows aside; and advocated the continued use of both private Masses and auricular confession. The passage of the Act was a complete triumph for the leader of the conservatives Stephen Gardiner, Bishop of Winchester, and his ally the Duke of Norfolk. It provided the framework for doctrinal orthodoxy for the remainder of Henry's reign, and the execution of Thomas Cromwell later that summer strengthened the position of the conservatives still further (**117, 138**).

Two days after Cromwell's execution, on 30 July 1539, three Protestants, one of them being the Cambridge leader Robert Barnes, were burnt for heresy on the very day that three of Catherine of Aragon's former supporters were executed for treason. In this cruel fashion the new regime demonstrated both its determination to eradicate heresy and to enforce loyalty to the Crown (**102**). Fortunately it moderated its policy in the following years but, though not repressive by contemporary standards, it did not deviate from orthodoxy. That orthodoxy was restated in 1543 with the publication of *The Necessary Doctrine and Erudition of a Christian Man*, compiled by the bishops with a preface supplied by the King. Known as *The King's Book*, it replaced *The Bishops' Book* of 1537, and not only reaffirmed traditional beliefs in such matters as masses for the dead, but also explicitly rejected Lutheran views on Justification by Faith and freedom of the will (**42**). Later in that year the conservatives had another success when Parliament passed an Act restricting the privilege of reading the Bible to those of the rank of merchant or gentleman and above. By this action the conservatives attempted to reverse the reformers' successes of the previous decade (**75**).

Though not immediately apparent, the events of the summer of 1543 probably marked the high point of the conservative reaction. The victory of Gardiner and his followers had placed Cranmer in a difficult position. He had not followed Shaxton and Latimer by resigning and, as far as we can tell, his views on the central doctrine of the Eucharist remained orthodox at this time, even if he did not wish to enforce that orthodoxy on everyone (**27**). During these years he turned his mind and his considerable literary gifts to liturgical reform. There was no departure from orthodoxy, but innovation came with the use of the vernacular in the English

Litany, published in 1544 and ordered to be used in churches. The Litany was followed in 1545 by *The King's Prymer* which attempted to provide a standard instruction manual for schoolmasters. Cranmer had even combined with conservatives like Edmund Bonner to produce a series of homilies designed for use by the less learned clergy. The *Book of Homilies* remained unpublished during Henry's reign and, though Cranmer experimented with an English order of Communion, the Latin Mass remained at the heart of the spiritual life of the Church during these years (**101**). It would be too deterministic to regard these liturgical experiments proposed by Cranmer as preparing the way for the events of the next reign, but 1543 saw another event which was to have important consequences in tipping the balance of power away from the conservatives.

In July of that year Henry VIII took as his sixth wife Catherine Parr and, once again, Protestants had a sympathiser at court. Some humble adherents still suffered, and the trial of the gentlewoman Anne Askew in 1546 brought heresy charges close to court [**doc. 12**] (**113**), but the presence of the new Queen offered some protection to Protestants and may also have revived the spirits of the isolated Archbishop Cranmer. Thus a reform group once again emerged at court and, most importantly, secured the education and upbringing of the young Prince Edward. The story of how this group, based in the Seymour and Dudley families, outmanoeuvred the conservatives is not altogether clear (**102**). The ageing King Henry surely assisted them when he excluded the powerful Bishop Gardiner from the Council of Regency, and they got unexpected help from the young Earl of Surrey, whose reckless behaviour brought him to the block and ruined the chances of his family, the Howards, at a critical juncture. The course of the Reformation was not decided solely by the power politics played out at court in the final stages of Henry's reign, but the eclipse of the conservative group in those months was a significant factor. It provided Thomas Cranmer with the opportunity to make up his own mind and to help establish the character of the Church which he had served as Archbishop in an apparently vacillating but none the less conscientious manner for fifteen years.

The chantries

The royal injunctions and articles of the 1530s and Latimer's sermon to Convocation had amounted to an attack on traditional piety which was only arrested by the victory of the conservatives in 1539. One of the principal objects of attack had been the elaborate intercessory machinery which the medieval Church had constructed to bridge the gap between this world and the next. Among the chief components of that machinery were the chantries, collegiate churches, religious guilds and hospitals or almshouses, which were founded chiefly for the purpose of providing a constant round of prayer for the souls of their founders, benefactors, and other patrons. Whatever charitable work they did in education or in poor relief was a secondary by-product of their intercessory role. This role was founded on belief in purgatory and on the assumption that 'the flames of purgatory' could be diminished or shortened as a result of particular acts of piety performed or paid for in this world (**73**). There is no doubt that purgatory held a powerful sway over the minds of contemporaries, and small bequests for masses and obits survive in great numbers until the 1550s (**142**). On the other hand the early sixteenth century saw a general decline in the number of chantry foundations in England except in some rural areas, particularly in the north and east, where additional clergy often provided pastoral help in large upland parishes [**doc. 14**].

The conservatives defended the theology on which the chantries were founded but, even so, from the 1530s some of the smaller institutions returned to lay hands or remained unfilled by clerics. Others, usually with larger incomes, were dissolved by royal initiative: eighteen in the years 1540–1543, ten in 1544 and twenty-seven in 1545·(**73**). In that year an Act of Parliament was passed enabling a further nineteen institutions to be annexed by the Crown on the entirely secular grounds of the need to raise money for wars with France and Scotland (**75**). This hardly conformed to the wishes of humanist reformers like Henry Brinkelow. He wrote of the chantries in 1543, asking that their property be put 'to the use of the Commonwealth, and unto the provision of the poor according to the doctrine of Scripture' (**2**).

It was the uses of the Commonwealth which were the declared intentions of the Act for Dissolving the Chantries; this was passed in the first Parliament of Edward's reign in 1547 (**6**). These public intentions were in harmony with the social gospel of the reformers, and there is no doubt that a greater proportion of the wealth of chantry and collegiate land was devoted to educational and charitable uses than had been the case with the monasteries. Schools were founded, or refounded in many market towns scattered throughout England, such as Newark, Maidstone and Crediton. Their existence represented a considerable social gain (**71, 90**). On the other hand, however, in many rural areas, such as in the Pennine parish of Deane, there was also a pastoral loss, for the dissolution of the chantries removed the provision for those additional and unbeneficed clergy who existed in great numbers in England and made a considerable contribution to pastoral care [**doc. 14**] (**122, 143**). The social and private advantages and disadvantages of the Chantries Act were discernible to the educated laity in 1547, but even more obvious were the doctrinal implications. The chantries were the concrete representation of a central doctrine in traditional religion – the belief in purgatory; their removal, viewed in the context of other events in 1547, clearly set the regime on the path towards Protestantism.

The beginnings of Protestant policy, 1547

The death of Henry VIII on 28 January 1547 had left the Protestant group in control of the new King, Edward VI, a boy of nine. The new regime, under the leadership of Edward Seymour (later Duke of Somerset), still had to contend with a powerful conservative group centred on the figure of Stephen Gardiner. The inclinations of Seymour, and the uncertainty of the balance of forces, meant that policy had to proceed cautiously and to be contained within the Council. There was no attempt to call Parliament, and so the earliest initiatives in matters of religion were taken under powers of visitation which broadly restated those of 1538, but with some important additions. All churches were required to have an English copy of Erasmus's *Paraphrases* on the Gospels, in addition to the Great Bible. This gloss on the Scriptures was unpopular with conservatives, who were also unconvinced of the desirability of preaching, which the parish clergy were ordered to provide at least once a quarter in their churches. Conservative doubts were increased by the requirement that, in the absence of preaching, the less able clergy should read from the *Book of Homilies* which had been recently published. Some of these homilies were written by Cranmer, and some of them, such as the one on faith which began 'The first entry unto God, good Christian people, is through faith: whereby, as it is declared in the last Sermon [on salvation] we be justified before God' (**13**, Cranmer vol. 2), came close to enunciating Lutheran views. These same injunctions also introduced English into the Mass for the first time by requiring that the Epistle and the Gospel, the biblical teaching texts of the Mass, should be read aloud in the vernacular. These additional clauses were not doctrinally radical, but they nevertheless represented a weakening of the doctrinal orthodoxy which the conservatives had established in the 1540s (**40, 69**). Gardiner recognised this and tried to prevent their implementation. Here he relied on his legal training and pointed out that the new measures contravened statute law as defined in the Six Articles. Gardiner, the arch-conservative defender of the royal supremacy, was using arguments which we are more accustomed to associate with Thomas Cromwell, and the implication was that the King himself (or in this case the Council of Regency) could not overrule the King in Parliament in matters touching religion (**87**). Clearly Parliament was the only instrument that could set aside statute law, and in November 1547 Parliament met.

In its first session Parliament continued the cautious policy of the Injunctions. The first Act of the new reign, the Act against Revilers, was carefully phrased to appeal to conservative opinion whilst at the same time establishing a central tenet of Protestant worship, the right of the laity to receive Communion in both kinds. Under Catholic worship, the clergy received both bread and wine at Communion, but the laity received only bread. The clause which appealed to the conservatives was that which maintained the real presence of Christ in the Eucharist, but it was as much directed against radicals as designed to appeal to traditionalists. The growth of Protestantism in the 1540s had produced a diversity of opinion about the sacrament of the altar, for the influence of the Swiss reformers had encouraged some men to deny any divine presence in the Eucharist and to think of it merely as a memorial of the Last Supper. Thus the Act was a somewhat optimistic attempt to prevent discussion of this central point of theology whilst, at the same time, introducing a new understanding of the ceremonial which incorporated that teaching. Parliament went on to pass the Chantries Act and also the Treasons Act, which swept away some of the more repressive measures of Henry's later years and removed the obstacles to reform which existed in the Act of Six Articles (**69**).

Cautious as the government was, by the end of 1547 it had become clear that a period of doctrinal change was in progress. Stephen Gardiner viewed these developments pessimistically, and from April 1548 his views came from the Tower, where he was imprisoned. A more optimistic position was taken by some continental reformers who, faced with the political consequences of the Catholic Counter-Reformation, came to England to study, teach and preach. Men like Peter Martyr from Italy or Martin Bucer from Strasbourg were to exert a profound influence on the ultimate character of English Protestantism through the young men they taught at the universities (**63, 98**). In the short term they offered support and advice to the new regime, but they were to be disappointed with the product of its early policy, the Prayer Book of 1549.

The first Prayer Book and the Act of Uniformity

The Parliamentary legislation of 1547 required further measures and explanations. A proclamation of March 1548 required that Cranmer's short *Order of Communion* be incorporated into the Mass when Communion in both kinds was administered to the laity. In this way English was introduced to the sacramental as well as to the teaching part of the Mass. This proclamation also stated publicly the government's determination to introduce further reforms and required the people in 'obedience and conformity to receive this our ordinance and most godly direction that we may be encouraged from time to time further to travail for the reformation and setting forth of our subjects, and for the advancement of true religion. Which thing we (by the help of God) most earnestly intend to bring to effect, willing all our subjects in the meantime to stay and quiet themselves with this our direction' (**12**). If the government hoped to keep innovations in check by promising change, then it was mistaken. By May 1548 Matins, Evensong, and the Mass itself were being conducted wholly in English at St Paul's and in other London churches (**42**).

In September of that year the bishops and other leading clerics met to devise a common order of prayer in English, and in December their deliberations came before Parliament. It was clear that the bishops were deeply divided on the crucial doctrine of the Eucharist, which lay at the very heart of religious worship. Many of the more senior of them held firmly to the Catholic doctrine of transubstantiation whilst others, led by Nicholas Ridley of Rochester, maintained that Christ was present in the Eucharist, but denied that the bread was physically transformed into the body of Christ. They viewed the real presence in a more mystical way. Cranmer had indeed been converted to this position by Ridley in 1546, but at this time, influenced by recently-arrived Calvinist reformers whose views denied any form of real presence in the Eucharist, he provided confused and contradictory leadership. It was, however, Ridley's view which became enshrined in *The Book of Common Prayer*. At the time – and ever since – confusion over the precise nature of the Eucharistic doctrine of 1549 was not uncommon. It certainly denied transubstantiation, but it maintained a belief in the divine presence in the sacrament. This presence was not expressed in Lutheran terms either, for their doctrine of consubstantiation required that the bread contained simultaneously the properties of bread and of the body of Christ. This was not so in Ridley's formula. Indeed its definition of a 'mystical presence' or 'divine influence' in the bread may have owed something to a tradition within the Church which descended from a ninth-century monk, Ratramnus, and which had subsequently found a following in some theological circles [**doc. 15a**] (**44**). Its traditional nature was recognised by the imprisoned Stephen Gardiner who stated that the new *Order of Communion* could be read as implying, though not fully expressing, traditional teaching on the Eucharist (**87**). However, he may have been straining the evidence, and the bishops remained divided. The common order of prayer, under the title *The Book of Common Prayer and Administration of Sacraments, and Other Rites and Ceremonies of the Church, after the use of the Church of England*, was enshrined in an Act of Uniformity which passed through Parliament on 21 January 1549 and was to take full effect on the following Whitsun Day. In the voting ten bishops were in favour of the Act and eight against (**69**).

Important as these theological discussions were, they were not the feature of the Prayer Book most apparent to the laity in general. All the laity would have placed most emphasis on the radical nature of the change from Latin to English, and some of them would also have been aware that the arrangement of the services, and in particular the Communion service, placed that radical departure within a liturgical framework which remained very close in structure to medieval Catholic precedent. There were only slight departures from the Sarum Use, the form of worship most common in late medieval England. The canon of the Mass was retained, though its sacrificial elements were replaced by prayers of offering and thanksgiving, and this represented an important link with tradition. On the Continent most Protestant liturgies, whether Lutheran or Calvinist, made no attempt to adapt the canon and had abandoned its use entirely. Understanding of the traditional elements in the Prayer Book required a level of theological knowledge beyond most of the laity, and possibly many of the lower clergy also. They were probably glad that the actual structure of the service to which they were accustomed had not altered dramatically (**44**).

Experiments with English liturgy had been common in London for over a year before *The Book of Common Prayer* came into use, but other parts of the country had not been so forward. In the south-west peninsula the introduction of English proved too much for the common people who, egged on by the parish clergy, rose in rebellion and laid siege to Exeter. The manifesto of the rebels demanded a return to Latin and to the orthodoxy enshrined in the Six Articles. The rising coincided with agrarian unrest in the West Country and, more importantly, in East Anglia. The government of the Duke of Somerset found itself in difficulties. These difficulties, sparked off in part by popular conservative opposition to the religious changes, had a paradoxical consequence (**36**). They contributed to the downfall of Somerset, who was replaced by John Dudley, Earl of Warwick. Dudley headed a regime more closely associated with those continental reformers who had been disappointed in the Prayer Book – not because of the changes it advocated, but because of its doctrinal and liturgical conservatism (**70**).

New influences and a new Prayer Book

Ever since the negotiations surrounding the divorce of Henry VIII and Catherine of Aragon, there had been fitful contact between English reformers and continental Protestant churches. When these contacts were conducted at an official level, they were usually confined to Lutheran princes and church leaders. However, none of the important European leaders of Lutheranism ever came to England and, indeed, the Lutherans themselves tended to concentrate on their own concerns in Saxony and did not actively pursue the international leadership of Protestantism. That leadership was to come from elsewhere: from the Geneva of Calvin and from the Strasbourg of Martin Bucer, where many Protestants had found, and were to continue to find, a refuge from persecution. One man who had passed through Strasbourg was the Italian Protestant Peter Martyr, who arrived in England in 1547 and was appointed Regius Professor of Divinity at Oxford in 1548. In that same year the Polish Protestant John à Lasco, at that time Superintendent of the Protestant churches in Friesland, paid a brief visit to England, before coming more permanently in 1550 when he assumed charge of the Protestant immigrant churches in London. It has been estimated that there were five thousand immigrants in the capital at this time, and many of them were Protestant. They were allowed to follow their native forms of worship which were often in advance of the order laid down in the 1549 Prayer Book. So it was that these Protestant churches provided a more radical example and stimulus to some English Protestants (**42**).

By far the most influential of these immigrants was Martin Bucer, the leader of the Strasbourg churches and a close friend of John Calvin. His temperament, however, was unlike that of Calvin, and his reputation for tolerance combined with a strong commitment to the Swiss reformation made Strasbourg a leading reform centre in the 1540s. Bucer shared with Cranmer an interest in and a talent for liturgical revision, and shortly after his arrival in England in April 1549 he was appointed Regius Professor of Divinity at Cambridge. From there he advised on the compilation of *The Ordinal* of 1550, which set out the order of service to be followed at the ordination of priests. The service followed the traditional rite quite closely, but announced its Protestantism unequivocally in the stress it placed on the function of the clergy. Where previously the new priest had been advised by his bishop to 'Receive authority to offer sacrifice and celebrate Mass both for the living and the dead', the new instructions were 'Take thou authority to preach the word of God and to minister the holy sacraments in the congregation' (**42**). In recognition of this important new stress on preaching, the ordinands were issued with Bibles in addition to the traditional chalice and paten used in the Eucharist (**63**).

The new ordinal was not acceptable to some conservatives, and Nicholas Heath, Bishop of Worcester, was deprived of his see for his opposition. Proceedings had already begun against other conservative bishops, resulting in deprivation or imprisonment for the most senior of them – Bonner of London, Gardiner of Winchester, and Tunstall of Durham (**70**). The process was not complete until 1552, but from the summer of 1550 government policy decisively tipped the balance of forces on the episcopal bench in favour of the Protestants. Some of these had been associated with and influenced by the Calvinist reformation and certainly held more radical views than Cranmer. One, John Hooper, only agreed to wear the traditional vestments at his consecration after being threatened with imprisonment, and rarely wore his episcopal insignia thereafter. His views on matters of ceremonial were extreme, but were to emerge again in the reign of Elizabeth. His pastoral commitment, however, ensured him a place as the prototype of the Protestant pastor-bishop in the English Church [**doc. 17**] (**137**).

The arrival of continental scholars and the decisive shift in favour of Protestantism among the bishops provided the background to the Prayer Book of 1552. Little is known of its origins, but it was certainly inspired by the criticisms of the 1549 Prayer Book made by Martin Bucer and published by him as a *Censura* soon after his arrival at Cambridge. The majority of Bucer's criticisms were incorporated in the revision, a draft of which was under discussion in January 1551. In its final form the 1552 Prayer Book retained the minor services from the earlier one, but made great and significant changes in the Order of Communion. Most obvious to the congregation would have been the replacement of the altar by a Communion table in a different and more accessible position. The unlearned would also have observed the substitution of the traditional vestments by a plain surplice. The more learned or more zealous layman would also have recognised that the structure of the service had been radically changed and that the canon had been redesigned to emphasise the congregational or communal features of the service. Finally, and doctrinally most important, the words at the administration of the sacrament were changed from 'The Body of Our Lord Jesus Christ which was given for thee, preserve thy body and soul unto everlasting life' to 'Take and eat this, in remembrance that Christ died for thee, and feed on him in thy heart by faith with thanksgiving' [**doc. 15a, b**). This new form, whilst it did not deny a belief in a real presence along the lines set out by Ridley in 1549, was also open to an interpretation acceptable to the most radical of the Swiss reformers who maintained that the Eucharist was merely a memorial of the Last Supper. Differences of view on the Eucharist could still be held by those adhering to the Prayer Book, but in 1552 these differences were within the Protestant camp and no longer between Protestant and Catholic (**40, 41**).

The new Prayer Book was passed by Parliament to come into use on 1 November 1552 and was therefore in use for less than a year before the death of Edward VI and the accession of Mary brought a return to Catholicism. It is difficult to assess its impact on the people at large (none of whom were provoked to rebellion however) and it is best viewed as defining the position of the Protestant leadership at that time. Its increasingly Calvinistic orientation was further underlined by the great codification of belief undertaken by Cranmer in 1552. This resulted in the promulgation of forty-two Articles in June 1553, less than one month before the end of the reign. The Articles, therefore, were a dead letter in the immediate future, but they formed the basis for the great codification of 1563, known as the Thirty-Nine Articles, and the doctrinal implications are discussed below (see page 59). The experiments of Edward VI's reign saw the Church of England retain its hierarchical structure, but emerge with an an unequivocally Protestant vernacular liturgy and an increasingly Calvinist theology (**70**).

Matters of law and discipline

Such fundamental changes in doctrine did not occur without incurring administrative and legal consequences for the Church. The Treasons Act of 1547 had removed the conservative restrictions on further reform, but that did not mean that toleration was extended to all. Other statutes and proclamations attempted to restrict discussion and, from 1549, uniformity was enforced by statute. The Acts of Uniformity allowed the church courts to proceed against offenders and to impose their traditional spiritual sanction of excommunication (**64**). These courts were supported by the secular courts which could, in some cases, impose life imprisonment for a third offence involving public opposition to the Prayer Book (**9**). The statutes, which were directed primarily against conservative opponents, were rarely invoked. Extreme radical opponents, such as the Anabaptists, fell foul of the heresy laws which were still in existence but, though others were harassed under these laws, only two heretics suffered death in Edward's reign (**92**). Nevertheless the Anabaptists, whose views included a denial of original sin and a dismissal of all scholarly theological learning in favour of inspiration from the spirit, caused concern to the authorities [**doc. 17**], and a number of the forty-two Articles devised in 1552 were directed against their teaching.

Within the ranks of the Church itself, the most notable innovation of these years was the legalising of clerical marriage in 1549 [**doc. 16**]. Clerical marriage had been advocated by continental reformers from the beginning and owed something to the Protestant view of the ministry as a pastoral rather than a sacramental institution. In England a few clerics had married in the 1530s, including Cranmer who married a niece of the Lutheran Andreas

Osiander whilst abroad. During the 1540s his marriage proved a serious threat to his position, but he was protected by his own discretion and by the friendship of the King (**101**). At the beginning of the new reign the question of a married clergy was soon broached but, having passed through Convocation and the Commons, proposals in favour were defeated by the Lords. In February 1549, however, the necessary support was forthcoming, and Parliament declared that the clergy were allowed to marry. Though there were regional variations, ranging from under 10 per cent in Yorkshire to over 30 per cent in London, many clergy took the opportunity to wed. For some it may have amounted to no more than regularising an already existing relationship, but others saw marriage as an opportunity to publicly declare their Protestant beliefs. The immediate consequences were not socially significant but many men were to find themselves in personal difficulties when the Marian regime revoked the statute and proceeded against married clergy in the courts (**43**). In the long term, however, clerical marriage was to have a profound effect upon English society, for clerical families came to form the first large professional class in provincial England.

Finally we must mention an unsuccessful scheme to codify church law in the light of the substantial institutional and doctrinal changes that had taken place since 1532. In 1549 a commission was established to look into the law of the Church, but was allowed to lapse. Cranmer's own scheme, which incorporated a few innovations such as annual meetings of the clergy and laity of each diocese, was essentially traditional and remained unpublished until 1571 when it appeared as *Reformatio Legum Ecclesiasticorum* (**64**). Of course the power of the papacy had been removed and the jurisdictional power of the Church ultimately rested in the Crown, but in other respects the church courts remained untouched. Those courts which had figured so prominently in anti-clerical propaganda in the 1520s and 1530s continued to exercise the same jurisdiction through the same agencies in the 1550s and, indeed, into the seventeenth century. What had changed was their power to instil fear and respect for their decisions. As time went on, increasing numbers of people either ignored their decisions in disciplinary matters or challenged them at common law. In practical terms the power of the Church to impose its will on the people was diminishing, but not before a vigorous and violent attempt was made to restore that power (**89**, Houlbrooke).

Protestantism in the reign of Mary

The Marian regime restored the papacy, revoked the legislation of Edward's reign, and revived the heresy laws, which were used against Protestants of all persuasions [**doc. 19**]. Bishops like Gardiner and Edmund Bonner, who had been deprived of their sees in Edward's reign, were active participants in this policy. For Protestants the restoration of Catholicism was a bitter reversal which produced three important consequences for the future development of Protestantism (**78**). Two of these derived from the persecution suffered by those Protestants who remained in England and the third was a result of the exile which many leading clerics and laymen chose.

Perhaps the most immediately significant consequence for Protestantism was the example of faithful suffering provided by the martyrs whom the Marian policy produced. Not only leading churchmen like Hooper, Ridley, and, finally, Cranmer, stood firm in the face of persecution and suffered death (**77**), but also many humble men and women, like George Eagles who was active around Colchester and was burnt at the stake for his Protestant beliefs [**doc. 20**]. Although small by European standards, the number of people put to death by the Marian regime ran into hundreds and produced in the next generation of Protestants a violent antipathy to all things Catholic and a firm belief in the Pope as Antichrist (**116**). In addition the martyrs provided that generation with an example of faithful suffering which was invaluable as propaganda. John Foxe, who had already been collecting details of Protestant sufferings before the end of Edward's reign, assembled data of all sorts on these martyrs and produced his *Actes and Monuments*, first published in English in 1563 [**doc. 23**]. This volume, with its detailed accounts of Protestant suffering, was to have a profound effect upon the religious attitudes of Englishmen for at least three hundred years (**57**).

Not all Protestants suffered death, and many congregations were able to survive undetected by the authorities. These groups were driven underground and often depended on the services of itinerant clergy. Groups like the one which met in several places in London, including on a ship near Rotherhithe called the Jesus Ship, for sermons, prayer, and Communion, were served by several different ministers, but they also owed their survival to their own sense of congregational solidarity and to the leadership of zealous laymen. Similar groups have been recorded in smaller towns, particularly in Kent and in East Anglia. Their existence showed that the 'Church of Christ' (as seen by Protestants) could survive in a hostile environment and did not depend upon the superstructure of a hierarchical national Church. The experience of these groups therefore established a tradition of congregational independence which, although often heterogeneous, was more in the mainstream of Protestantism than the earlier example of the Anabaptists had been. This tradition continued to have a respectable following among a minority of members in the Elizabethan Church (**132**).

Persecution, therefore, led to a different concept of 'the Church' from that which had evolved with official support in the more sympathetic environment of Edwardian England. The tensions that existed as a result of these differing views did not emerge into the open until after 1570.

A more immediate influence on the attitudes of leading English Protestants in matters of church order and government was the experience of exile. Some eight hundred people, including some prominent laymen and many graduate clergymen and students, chose exile. Once in exile, principally at Strasbourg, Geneva and Frankfurt, these English Protestants came into contact with reformed churches which had abandoned episcopacy and which had evolved a church order involving greater lay participation in the liturgy and the pastoral work of the Church (**53**). In theological matters exile confirmed the Calvinist orientation of English Protestantism which had become apparent by the end of Edward's reign. In matters of liturgy and church government many exiles became convinced that these non-episcopal congregations represented the fullest and most complete expression of Protestant theology. On these matters, however, there was no unanimity among the exiles and at Frankfurt their differences spilled over into dissension. The English Protestants in the city had, on the advice of William Whittingham, remodelled the 1552 Prayer Book along more Calvinist lines and had exhorted exiles elsewhere to do the same. Not all of their compatriots were enthusiastic about the new form of worship, but under the leadership of John Knox the radicals of Frankfurt maintained their opposition to those aspects of the 1552 Prayer Book which they deemed papistical, in particular the Litany and the simplified vestments. There was, however, a group at Frankfurt who wished to worship in accordance with the Prayer Book and the arrival of Richard Cox in 1555 provided them with vigorous leadership. After some quarrelling, some doctrinal discussion, and not a little political manoeuvring, the defenders of the Prayer Book, led by Cox, gained the support of the civic authorities, and Knox left for Geneva with some of his supporters. When Mary died and the Protestant Elizabeth succeeded to the throne at the end of 1558, the exiles placed their common Calvinist theology before these differences and, with varying degrees of willingness, they returned to assume leadership of the Elizabethan Church. Differences over matters of government and ceremonial were buried in order to further the common cause, but the truce proved temporary and these issues were to reappear in the English Church from the mid-1560s (**42**).

The experience of persecution under Mary revealed in microcosm the underlying tensions within English Protestantism over matters of church order and discipline. In that sense the reign was a pointer to future difficulties. It was also, however, a testimony to past achievement. The very extent of the persecution and the impressive number of able men and women who fled to the Continent indicated that Protestantism was no longer confined to a few zealots.

4 A Church and Nation half-reformed? The Settlement, 1558–1570

The accession of Elizabeth in November 1558 brought to an end the religious policy of her half-sister, and most contemporaries involved in political life had anticipated that this would be the case. Elizabeth had been educated among the Cambridge group of humanist scholars from which also emerged men such as William Cecil, Nicholas Bacon and John Aylmer who were to play a major role in the religious settlement of 1559 and its consolidation during the following decades (**65**). That the new regime would favour a settlement on Protestant lines was well-known, but the particular character of its Protestantism and whether its supporters would be able to carry their policy through Parliament and the political nation were both less certain. Opposition from those who had supported Mary and indifference from many other quarters were serious barriers to the achievement of any Protestant settlement; and it was the first task of the new regime to develop a strategy to overcome these. This was not an easy task, not only because of the strength of the opposition, but also because of the political inexperience of many of the key advisers of the Queen ('Young folks, heretics' in the words of the Spanish Ambassador) and because the experiences of martyrdom, persecution and exile in Mary's reign had created within Protestant ranks a disparate range of contacts and experience resulting in differing views about the nature and character of a reformed Church. In such circumstances the development of an effective and widely-supported strategy was difficult, but for the new regime it was the essential starting point on its religious agenda; and religion was, for most of them, the starting point of politics.

The settlement in Parliament

The religious settlement of Elizabeth, long characterised by the description '*via media*', had the status for many generations as the foundation of the Anglican Church. The Acts of Supremacy and Uniformity and the Royal Injunctions of 1559 were, with the addition of the Thirty-Nine Articles of 1563 and the Authorised Version of the Bible of 1611, the distinctive attributes of Anglicanism, an episcopal Protestantism purged of the errors of Rome yet free from the excesses of the more radical Protestant sects. Consequently a view of the settlement emerged early in this century which suggested that the events of 1559 resulted from the wish of Elizabeth, supported by the House of Commons, to unite the Church under the royal supremacy, with a form of worship based on the 1552 Prayer Book, and her and her counsellors' need to compromise with conservative and Catholic peers who, with the surviving Marian bishops, sought to defeat the settlement in the House of Lords. The picture that was painted was, therefore, one of compromise between Elizabeth and her supporters and their conservative opponents (**52**).

This picture was dramatically altered by the work published by Sir John Neale in the 1950s on the Parliaments of Elizabeth. From his work a totally different picture emerged, of a cautious and conservative Queen manoeuvred against her will into more radical positions by an organised group of radical MPs, 'the Puritan choir'. In Neale's view, Elizabeth, concerned about the international implications of an unequivocally Protestant settlement, would have been happy simply with restoring the royal supremacy but, having concluded peace with France, was prepared to consider an Act of Uniformity also. According to Neale, Elizabeth favoured the more conservative 1549 Prayer Book, but was faced with opposition from some members of the House of Commons who, influenced by the views of returning clergy like Percival Wiburn, desired a Prayer Book more radical than that of 1552, and along Calvinist lines as produced by the exiles in Frankfurt. It was in attempting to settle this conflict and in recognition of the desperate need of the Church for able leadership that Elizabeth compromised on the Act of Uniformity of 1559, the ambiguities of which resulted in conflict between the establishment and the Puritans for the next half-century and beyond. Thus, in Neale's view, the settlement of 1559 was not one made by a Protestant regime struggling with its conservative opponents, but a temporary settlement between a conservative Queen and some of her more radical Protestant supporters (**88**).

This latter view became the accepted orthodoxy for the next generation, but recent work has suggested that the two interpretations are not mutually exclusive; the Queen did have to face important opponents with vested interests in a conservative settlement, and at the same time had to cope with the expectations of those who had suffered under Mary or had seen the fully reformed churches of the Continent. The settlement did not result from compromise with any one group, but was a delicate operation to balance a variety of forces.

On the death of Mary the immediate task was not one of dealing with opposition but of preparing the groundwork for change. Within a week Dr William Bill, a known Protestant, preached the Paul's Cross sermon, and though he was required not to 'stir any dispute', his very presence indicated that change was in the air. By Christmas it was common knowledge in court and diplomatic circles that English had been introduced in part to the services in the Chapel Royal, where 'A litany . . . which used to be sung in the time of King Edward, in which no saints at all are mentioned' was rumoured to be in use (**56**, Jones). A royal proclamation of 28 December 1558 sought to forbid unlicensed preaching (much of it being done by Protestant ministers in and around London) for the sake of preventing 'unfruitful dispute in matters of religion' among the common sort; but it also promised those Protestants that the Queen desired reform 'in matters and ceremonies of religion, the true advancement wherof . . . her majesty most desireth and meaneth effectually by all manner of means possible to procure and to restore to this her realm' (**12**). By the end of the year it was clear that reform was intended, but the work of Cecil and Elizabeth, both in treating with the Spanish abroad and in urging caution at home, ensured that opposition among the Catholic laity and clergy was restrained.

In these circumstances Parliament met in January 1559 and by the end of April had passed the Acts of Supremacy and Uniformity establishing the settlement of religion. In the House of Commons both Catholics and radical Protestants were small in number, and recent research does not suggest that the Protestants organised opposition to the policies of the Crown. In 1559 most would have endorsed the judgement of John Jewel, who commented, 'We have a wise and religious Queen, and one who is favourably and propitiously disposed towards us' (**22**). The situation in the House of Lords was very different; here the Catholics, through the Marian bishops, were in a narrow majority, and the government required considerable political skill in order to achieve its aims.

The first Supremacy Bill included the title 'Supreme Head' and also had appended to it a form of service closely resembling that of the 1552 Prayer Book. It passed the Commons, but was rejected by the Lords who modified the terms of the Supremacy and removed all references to the order of service. The Commons responded by seeking to pass a Bill for toleration of 'that Religion used in Kyng Edward's last year', but Protestants had to content themselves with a proclamation of 22 March permitting the reception of Communion in both kinds (**67**). During the Easter recess the government scored an important public victory against the Catholics as a result of a disputation between eight Protestant and eight Catholic divines, whilst the signing of the peace treaty with France on 24 March eased international pressure on the new regime.

With its position now stronger, the government separated the Acts of Supremacy and Uniformity, concentrating the former on the constitutional position of the monarch in the Church. The title was changed from 'Supreme Head' to 'Supreme Governor', a compromise suggested by a returned exile, Thomas Lever, which not only neutralised the opposition of the Catholics, but also quelled the doubts about the headship among some Protestants. In addition, the Act included clauses licensing the reception of Communion in both kinds and repealing the heresy laws recently revived by Mary.

The Act of Uniformity when it was introduced was a direct descendant of the Acts of Edward VI, and eleven of the fourteen sections are direct copies from earlier Acts [**doc. 21**]. There are only two important differences between the Prayer Book established by this Act and its predecessor of 1552: the rubric concerning ornaments and the change of wording at the Communion. The most recent scholarship suggests that both these changes were made by the Queen and her advisors. The decision to recommend the ornaments of the 1549 Prayer Book disappointed the more radical Protestants, but the wording of the Act was such that the possibility of further change was held out. This clause 'until other order shall be therein taken by the authority of the Queen's Majesty with the advice of her commissioners appointed', which was prefaced to the printed Prayer Book, was later to be a major area of dispute. In the short term it satisfied the radicals, whilst the main clauses of the bill ensured a stability and order in the worship of the Church to which the Queen, by both temperament and the requirements of politics, was sympathetic (**58**).

The matter of the wording of the Communion was theologically a more fundamental issue and likely to prove a greater stumbling block to the passage of the bill. The change in the wording linked the formula of 1549 with that of 1552 as follows: 'The body of our Lord Jesus Christ which was given for thee, preserve thy body and soul unto everlasting life: and take and eat this, in remembrance that Christ died for thee, and feed on him in thine heart by faith, with thanksgiving' [**doc. 15c**]. This attempt at reconciling very differing views of the nature of the Eucharist aroused the opposition of some Protestants in the Commons, but to the Lords it showed enough of the old Catholic doctrine to get the support of some of the lay conservatives. The importance of this support was clear from the final vote in the Lords which saw the passage of the Act of Uniformity achieved by a narrow majority of three, with all the bishops present voting against (**67**).

The skill of the government in managing this settlement did not depend entirely on liturgical concessions and theological niceties; politics also played its part, as in the appointments of councillors and the conduct of the Easter disputation. The religious settlement passed into law without the support of any bishop or leader of the established Church and over the head of a protesting Convocation. In such circumstances any settlement would have had to contain elements of compromise. Recent research suggests that, when such compromises were made, they were more often directed towards conservative opponents than towards radical Protestants. As a compromise it was a brilliant one, particularly in its statement on the Eucharist, but like many compromises it gained acceptance in some quarters because its status was uncertain and its permanence far from guaranteed. Having won the battle in Parliament, the government now had to establish the religious character of the new regime and win the battle for the hearts of the people.

Consolidating the settlement

The three main characteristics of the settlement have been noted and discussed in the account of the parliamentary legislation, but the Acts of Supremacy and Uniformity contained other clauses which need to be considered if we are to understand the nature of the settlement more fully. The Supremacy Act revived most of the legislation of the Reformation Parliament of Henry VIII and, although the Queen did not have the title 'Supreme Head', she did retain the right to hold a visitation of the Church through commissioners appointed for that purpose: indeed, a visitation was embarked upon in the same year. In addition, the Queen was empowered to appoint a more permanent court of commissioners, both laymen and clerics, to assist with the government of the Church. These commissioners had greater powers than the normal church courts and in the north of England were active in prosecuting prominent Catholic sympathisers whose local influence rendered them immune from prosecution by diocesan officials (**39**).

The Uniformity Act included clauses relating to its enforcement, especially the famous clause imposing the 12*d.* fine for the benefit of the poor on persons who absented themselves from church. It also introduced severer penalties than earlier legislation for those speaking against the *Book of Common Prayer*, and in difficult cases encouraged the bishops to seek the assistance of the secular courts [**doc. 21**].

In the face of this settlement, the bishops who had opposed it so vigorously in Parliament resigned. Such a total rejection of the settlement by the leaders of the Church might have created great difficulties for the new regime but, if that was the intention of the Marian bishops, it failed. Their example was not followed by the majority of the lower clergy, only some 300 of whom resigned or were deprived of office. These numbers were not insignificant, including as they did some influential men, but they did not pose insurmountable problems for the regime; rather they gave it the opportunity of placing able Protestants in important places in the Church. During the next three years these new appointments were completed. Most important of all was the appointment of Matthew Parker, once Anne Boleyn's chaplain, who with some reluctance agreed to become Archbishop of Canterbury. Parker's reluctance was due to his personal inclinations rather than to doctrinal objections (**26**), but other leaders of the new Church such as Edwin Sandys, who had seen the reformed churches of the Continent in exile under Mary, had serious qualms about assuming the office of episcopacy, an office which many continental churches had abolished. Some men, such as Laurence Humphrey, went so far as to refuse, preferring instead to take important university posts (**13**, Zurich letters). There is no doubt that, in the higher offices of the Church, the new regime was fortunate in having able and committed Protestants to fill the episcopal bench. Many of them, however, combined a thankfulness for the Protestant settlement with a desire for further, if gradual, reform. The pastoral contribution of such men to the newly-established Church cannot be underestimated (**89**, Houlbrooke). This was not the case with the lower clergy.

The settlement, coming as it did at the end of a generation of chopping and changing in religious affairs, landed on an already demoralised clerical profession and at first the new Church had great difficulty in finding able men willing to take up the ministry. The early years of the reign were marked therefore by a pastoral problem in the parishes, a shortage of suitable clergy which not only left congregations without a resident clergyman but also required that, in order to meet the emergency, standards of learning and sometimes of life were lowered in the case of candidates (**89**, O'Day). These deficiencies, and the existence of luke-warm and even antagonistic conservative ex-Marian priests among the parochial clergy (**133**), ensured that the swift victory of the government at the centre was not repeated so easily in the nation at large. A slow and difficult process of evangelisation was required.

During the summer of 1559, however, these problems lay in the future. The immediate concern, following the resignation of the bishops, was to ensure that the new legislation was carried into effect. A royal visitation to bring churches and clergy into line was embarked upon. A set of Injunctions, numbering fifty-seven in all and covering almost all aspects of parish life, were administered to parochial officers who had to answer them under oath. These Injunctions required the removal of shrines and images and other liturgical trappings of the old religion, and insisted that altars be replaced by communion tables (which had to be 'decently made'), but left the matter of clerical dress ambiguous. Although the new Queen was not personally a champion of clerical marriage, the Injunctions established it as lawful once more [**doc. 16b**] (**9**). By October the visitation was completed, but how far it had been effective remained open to question. When Edmund Grindal moved from London to become Archbishop of York in 1570, he was horrified at the extent to which parish churches there retained fittings appropriate to the old religion, and he had to issue an order reminding churchwardens of the need to comply with the 1559 Injunctions (**32**). A similar situation obtained in the south-west (**36**). The Injunctions therefore marked no more than a first step on the long road towards reformation in the parishes.

So far we have concentrated on the means by which the government sought to establish the new religion and make it known and adhered to within its own country. There was also a need to provide a justification of the settlement to an international audience of both Protestants and Catholics, all of whom were watching affairs in England closely. This justification was provided by a returned exile, John Jewel, who had been appointed Bishop of Salisbury in 1560. He published a Latin text in 1562, *Apologia Ecclesiae Anglicanae*, which set out for both Catholics and Protestants a statement of the nature of the religious settlement and the sources of its authority. To Jewel, echoing the legislation of 1559, the Church of England was based on the Scriptures and on the Fathers of the Primitive Church, and it recognised the first four Councils of the Church as its sources of authority. Jewel also discussed the threefold ministry of bishops, priests and deacons, the role of Christ as the only mediator between God and man, and the doctrine of Justification by Faith. Faith was central to the understanding of the Eucharist, Jewel wrote: 'We affirm that bread and wine are holy and heavenly mysteries of the body and blood of Christ, and that by them Christ himself, being the true bread of eternal life, is so presently given to us as that by faith we verily receive his body and blood. Yet say we not this so as though we thought that the very nature of bread is changed . . .'. In other sections of the book, Jewel defended the rites and ceremonies of the Church, refuted the charge that England had 'fallen into sundry sects', and attacked the immorality of the Roman Church as he saw it. The volume became the standard defence of the Church of England for the next thirty years, and two translations into English had appeared by 1564 [**doc. 22**]. It was also translated into several European languages, and the exiled Catholics on the Continent, against whom the work was chiefly directed, wrote forty-one volumes opposing Jewel's defence before 1568 (**22, 13**, Jewel).

If Jewel laid the theoretical groundwork of the established Church before an international audience, another book, first published in English in 1563, laid the history of the struggles and sufferings of English Protestants before the nation. John Foxe's *Actes and Monuments*, more popularly known as the *Book of Martyrs*, was to become one of the most influential books on English Protestantism for the next three hundred years (**7**). Its immediate impact is less easy to assess, but the vivid use of illustrative material made it accessible to a wide readership [**doc. 23**]. Though the work recounted the sufferings of the reformers at the hands of the papists [**doc. 20**], Foxe himself preferred not to dwell on suffering and persecution in the hope of revenge, but sought to draw lessons for toleration, at least within the Protestant churches, from recent history (**57**).

We have seen how the senior posts in the new Church were

staffed by able men, some of whom had scruples about holding the offices they did. The Protestants in 1559 had supported the Queen and government, but at the same time many influential clergy expected that the terms of the settlement would be revised in due course. In 1563 a new Parliament and Convocation were called, and it was in the course of their meetings that the determination of the Queen to stay with the terms of the 1559 settlement became apparent. This realisation put to the test the alliance of the government and the new bishops with more radical reformers, and the failure of the more militant members of Convocation to achieve further liturgical and disciplinary reform marked the beginning of conflict between the established Church and its loyal but dissatisfied Protestant critics, later to be given the name of Puritans. The bishops led the discussion and succeeded in getting the agreement of most members of Convocation to a series of articles which clarified fundamental areas of doctrine, eliminated trivial condemnations of sectarian beliefs, emphasised their rejection of Roman Catholicism, authorised a new *Book of Homilies* for non-preaching clergy, and clarified the role of the Supreme Governor. Some difficulty remained over the article on the Eucharist and so, in their original form, thirty-eight Articles were authorised (**58**). Eight years later, in 1571, the Articles were again approved, and this time the one concerning the Eucharist, which did not rule out the belief in a real spiritual presence in the sacrament, was also accepted. The Thirty-Nine Articles were given the force of statute law by Parliament and became the fundamental confession of faith of the English Church (**3, 88**).

The years between 1559 and 1571, therefore, saw the emergence of the doctrinal beliefs of the established Church and also the confirmation of its church order as an episcopal one. The story of this achievement shows that there was conservative opposition to the doctrine and radical opposition to the church order, and the strength of these two groups needs to be considered. However, it is also important to remember that the Queen set great store by stability, at least in the outward forms of religious life, and that in so doing she had made the transition from Marian Catholicism to Elizabethan Protestantism an outwardly gentle one for the average English church-goer (**40**). It is legitimate and necessary to consider the critics of the settlement, but it is also worth recalling that the longer it endured, the more the settlement could expect acquiescence and even sympathetic support from the ordinary people. As time went on, it also began to attract intellectual defenders like John Aylmer and John Whitgift, who were to play an important part in defending the settlement in the decades after 1570.

Conservatives and Catholics

The collapse of conservative opposition at home in 1559 was accompanied by the failure of the Catholic church, involved in its own reformation at the Council of Trent, to mobilise international opinion against the new regime (**23**). It was not until 1562 that the Pope forbade Catholics to attend the new services, and that order was not made public in England until 1566 (**45, 55**). This delay gave the new regime a vital opportunity to establish itself, and the decade following 1559 has been seen by some historians as marking the virtual collapse of traditional English Catholicism (**23**). Recent studies have suggested, however, that although Catholicism was in a bad way, it was not moribund. Marian priests who had been removed at the settlement were sustaining congregations not only in traditional strongholds such as Lancashire (**55, 127, 133**), but also in counties like Sussex, where in 1564 the Bishop of Chichester despaired of winning over the multitude until more members of the gentry had been persuaded to support the settlement (**82**).

This sort of survival was superficially similar to the position of Protestantism under Mary, but with two crucial differences. Firstly, the new regime was fairly tolerant towards Catholics, and in many areas throughout the 1560s Catholics, or their sympathisers, continued to serve as Justices of the Peace or in other government commissions (**20, 82, 105**). Secondly, English Catholics at this time had little positive leadership from or contact with the Catholic church; thus their religion remained isolated and backward-looking, not fired with evangelical zeal. The ending of the Council of Trent and the founding of a college for the training of English Catholic missionaries at Douai in France changed all that. In addition, international political developments surrounding the figure of Mary Queen of Scots led to a period of crisis between 1568 and 1571 which undermined the relationship between the Elizabethan state and its Catholic subjects.

These events, comprising an abortive marriage alliance between Mary Queen of Scots and the Duke of Norfolk, a half-hearted and easily-suppressed rising of some of the northern gentry under the Earls of Northumberland and Westmorland, and the issue of a

Papal Bull excommunicating Elizabeth [**doc. 26**], were poorly co-ordinated by the Catholics and have been detailed by other volumes in this series (**45, 51**). The result was that the policy of gradually absorbing Catholics into local government was abandoned after 1570. The work of the missionary priests created a new revived Catholicism which either emerged as a household-based spirituality distinct from the mainstream of English life or was actively hostile, if not subversive, to the Elizabethan regime (**23**).

Protestant activists

As we have seen, the experience of exile during Mary's reign had brought many men and women into contact with the continental churches reformed on Calvinist principles at Strasbourg, Geneva and Frankfurt. The English exiles differed in their response to these models, but many saw them as desirable ambitions for a Protestant religion (**13**, Original Letters). On their return to England some of the clerical leaders, such as Edmund Grindal, were persuaded to accept posts of responsibility in the new Church and even to serve as bishops, an office which a fully-fledged Calvinist church had abolished as popish (**32, 33**). Among the returning exiles there were others whose scruples would not permit them to accept bish-oprics and whose attitude to the terms of the Elizabethan settle-ment remained ambivalent. Welcoming the return to Protestantism itself, they remained cool, regarding the Prayer Book and Injunc-tions of 1559 as no more than preliminary steps on the road to full reformation. They were a minority, but they had some influential lay support in men like Anthony Cooke, father-in-law to William Cecil, and Francis Russell, Earl of Bedford, and they also included among their numbers some distinguished individuals whose personal reputations for learning and preaching ensured that they would have an important influence on the character of the new Church.

Laurence Humphrey, as President of Magdalen College, Oxford, was in a position to influence the next generation of clergy, whilst others such as Thomas Lever, whose advice had been instru-mental in influencing Elizabeth to assume the title of 'Supreme Governor', accepted preaching posts in important provincial towns. Lever became town preacher at Coventry, itself a cathedral city with two parish churches, and as such remained independent of the formal structures of the Church, depending for his living on the voluntary subscriptions of the townspeople. As preacher he was not required to perform the sacramental duties of the ministry, such as the administration of Communion, and so remained at some distance from the formal life of the new Church whilst at the same time recognising that he was working alongside it in bringing the gospel to the people. The Church leadership knew that men like Lever were essential to its work of evangelisation and eventually, in 1561, at the suggestion of his bishop, he became an archdeacon (**13**, *Zurich Letters*, **33**). In the early part of Elizabeth's reign therefore the tensions between the government and the more radical clergy were overcome by the pressing needs for preaching and gaining acceptance of the new religion. Even so the tensions were there, and men such as Lever and William Whittingham – an exile in Geneva who had been called to the ministry by the exiled congregation there without episcopal ordination, but who nevertheless later became Dean of Durham – represented an important category of radical clergy. They were mostly former exiles, and they anticipated that there would be a speedy advance towards a more fully Calvinist form of church order. In 1564 Lever and Whittingham, along with twenty-six others, were mentioned to Robert Dudley (later Earl of Leicester) as 'godly preachers which have utterly forsaken Antichrist and all his Romish rags', unlike 'the lord bishops and others that for worldly respects receive and allow them' (**33**).

Some bishops such as Edmund Grindal, who as Bishop of London secured four out of five archdeaconries and the chancellorship of his diocese for returned exiles (**32**), shared this hope of further reform, but, as the 1564 list indicates, disagreement was beginning to emerge between the bishops and the more radical clergy about the means by which any reform might proceed. The chief bone of contention in the early years of the reign centred on the requirement of the 1559 Injunctions that clergy should wear the surplice at service and a distinctive clerical dress at other times. To the radicals this smacked of popery, and they turned to the continental Protestant leaders, particularly those in Zurich, for advice (**13**, *Zurich Letters*). Late in 1564 a conference between the bishops and those whose scruples were offended by the vestments was arranged, but only a qualified agreement was reached. The problem was that the bishops saw vestments as an 'indifferent' rather than a necessary part of the church order, but nevertheless they required that, for the sake of decency and uniformity, clergy should wear them. To the radicals, vestments were either antichristian and should therefore be rejected, or they were 'matters indifferent' and as such should certainly not be enforced (**33**).

In 1565 the Queen intervened with a letter to Archbishop Parker publicly rebuking the bishops for permitting 'varieties, novelties and diversities' to grow up in the rites and ceremonies of the Church and demanding that steps be taken to impose some uniformity. Within a week the Archbishop required all bishops to report on the disorders and to use the church courts to suppress them (**13**, Parker). Some of the bishops were themselves troubled by this request; they disliked the vestments, but were persuaded that they were not idolatrous in themselves and could be imposed for the sake of order. They too wrote to the Zurich pastors for advice, sadly reflecting that 'our little flock has divided itself into two parties' (**13**, Zurich Letters). In March 1565 twenty of the radical clergy appealed to the Ecclesiastical Commissioners, asking to be excused from conforming to the orders and, for the rest of the year, uncertainty prevailed. In March 1566, however, the orders of the Archbishop requiring uniformity of practice, known as the Advertisements, were published and crisis could no longer be averted [**doc. 24**]. That crisis took place in London, which at this stage set the tone in matters of religion for the country as a whole. At the end of March, 110 clergy were summoned to Lambeth and ordered to comply with the Advertisements. Thirty-seven declined to do so, were suspended and threatened with deprivation. Among them were such distinguished figures as John Foxe the martyrologist. On the eve of Easter, the high point of the liturgical year, one-third of the London parishes were deprived of their ministers and, even worse, those acted against were, in the eyes of their congregations, the most diligent among the clergy (**33**).

The way in which the more radical of the suspended clergy chose to defend themselves was through the publication of tracts directed against the surplice and setting out their position on vestments. Thus began the first skirmish in the pamphlet warfare between the establishment and the Puritans which was to break out at regular intervals over the next eighty years. In the course of this exchange relations between the parties deteriorated and even a moderate like Anthony Gilby of Ashby-de-la-Zouch was to take up the pen in controversy, asking the 'proud prelates' to repent and no longer to enforce the vestments, which he described as 'this filthy ware' (**33**). It is true that Gilby's views remained private and, though written in 1566, were not published until 1573, but others, such as

Robert Crowley, were less inhibited in their criticisms (**33**). Both parties again appealed to their continental brethren and met with mixed receptions. Heinrich Bullinger at Zurich came down on the side of uniformity and good order, warning the Puritans not to conceal 'a contentious spirit under the name of conscience', but the Puritans received more support from Theodore Beza at Geneva, and also from Bullinger's colleague at Zurich, Rudolph Gualter (**13**, Zurich Letters). However, Grindal and Parker were not moved from their resolve, and by July 1566 only eight beneficed clergy, three parish lecturers and three or four curates were still holding out against the vestments. The others had succumbed or had been brought round to accepting the need for uniformity. The remaining few were deprived, though some, once removed from London, found church livings in the provinces away from the sensitive political atmosphere of the capital (**33**). The dispute over vestments and the actions of the bishops made clear the differences that existed among Protestants over the status of the Elizabethan settlement. At this stage those differences seemed to recall past divisions during the period of exile, rather than to point to fundamental disagreements over the nature of a properly reformed Church (**35**). Most of the dissidents were brought to conformity, but some of the clergy were driven out of the Church and others continued to hope for further reform. These individuals, together with a new generation of graduates taught by men like Laurence Humphrey, were to disagree not only about strategy but about the whole structure of ecclesiastical order.

In the years immediately following the Vestiarian Controversy, as the events of 1566 came to be called, the more intransigent radicals in London formed a separatist congregation meeting at Plumbers Hall in the city; the ministers of the congregation looked towards the tradition of the gathered churches that had existed in London during the persecutions of Mary's reign (**132**) and to the model of church order that some of them had experienced in exile in Geneva [**doc. 25**]. Thomas Wood, formerly an elder in the Geneva church, had begun to hold meetings with those clergy who had been deprived of office for refusing the surplice and, faced with what they considered to be the intolerance of the bishops, this group began to question more openly the scriptural authority for an episcopal Church (**33, 104**). These men had the experience of exile under Mary and, in the 1560s, the example of the French church for Protestant refugees in London as an alternative form of church government, a form based on congregations governed by pastors and elders who were called and elected by their flocks. Whilst this group was active in London, a Cambridge divine, Thomas Cartwright, delivered a series of lectures on the Acts of the Apostles early in 1570 in the course of which he challenged the biblical basis for episcopal government and advocated what came to be known as a Presbyterian form of church order similar to that which existed in Geneva and which had recently been established in Scotland.

Cartwright was forced to leave Cambridge and he went to Geneva, but the impact of his lectures was not so easily dismissed (**96**). The Protestant settlement had been established for ten years now and many were disappointed at the slow progress that had been made. Many abuses remained within the Church – for example, non-resident and non-preaching clergy, pluralism among careerist clerics, and the system of church courts – in much the same form as in Henry VIII's time. Indeed it must have looked to the radicals as if the complaints made by Colet in his sermon of 1511 were still justified [**doc. 1**]. Moreover the task of evangelising the nation was proving more difficult than had been anticipated; many of the parochial clergy still survived from Mary's reign and were unsympathetic to the new regime (**133**), the upheaval in religious policy during the previous generations had left many people confused and uncertain as to what was official policy, and the numbers of able and learned clergy fitted for preaching the gospel were small. It was of course unrealistic to expect the Reformation to be completed so quickly, but the events of 1566 led some Protestants to believe that the bishops were, by their policies, at least partly responsible for the delay. Even more importantly, by their actions the bishops appeared to be opposing and depriving the very clergy and ministers who were most zealous for the cause of Protestantism. These views began to gain a following among influential laymen, some of whom may have attended lectures at Cambridge and others of whom would have heard radicals preaching sermons in the capital whilst they were law students at the Inns of Court.

Thus it was that some of the radicals, organised by John Field, a deprived London minister, turned their hopes for further reformation away from the bishops and towards Parliament, where they had support from some MPs. By the time Parliament assembled in April 1571 the radicals had devised a programme for further reform in consultation with some of the Commons, one of whom introduced a bill for the removal from the *Book of Common Prayer* of all objectionable rites and ceremonies, including the wearing of the surplice. The bishops and the Parliamentary supporters of the radicals could not agree, and the bishops went on the offensive, summoning some of the radical ringleaders before the High Commission. Parliament was dissolved without agreement being reached (**33, 88**), but the return of Thomas Cartwright from Geneva, and the announcement of a new Parliament for 1572 to consider the fate of the Catholic Duke of Norfolk and Mary Queen of Scots, gave a fresh opportunity for Field and his friends to organise. Soon after Parliament assembled, he and his associates published *An Admonition to Parliament*, a tract against the established Church more polemical than anything that had gone before. It claimed that England was still far from having a 'Church rightly reformed according to the prescripts of God's word' and listed the popish abuses that remained, including the Prayer Book, 'culled and picked out of that popish dunghill, the Mass book'; the Church courts, 'a petty little stinking ditch that floweth out of that former great puddle'; and bishops, who were said to be 'Antichristian and devilish and contrary to the Scriptures' [**doc. 27**].

The tone of the *Admonition* was aggressive and offensive, and its publication marked the destruction of any common ground linking the bishops and the most extreme radicals [**doc. 28**]. Yet between these two poles were many men like Thomas Lever and Thomas Sampson, who sympathised with both parties, whilst other committed Protestants such as Edward Dering, a Fellow of Christ's College, Cambridge, until he resigned in 1570 and moved to London, regretted the dissension caused by the controversy. Dering himself had no doubt that the Church of England still contained many evils, but they did not justify the violence of Field's polemic. In 1570 Dering wrote, 'I have never broken the peace of the Church, neither for cap nor surplice, for archbishop or bishop', and his view was shared by many (**34**).

Not all Puritans, therefore, would go as far as Field and Wilcox, his associate in writing the *Admonition*, but the publication of that tract and the emergence of a group of clergy with strong Presbyterian sympathies meant that, in the two generations following 1570, the energies of the established Church were occupied as much in combating radical elements within its fold as in struggling with those forces of Antichrist which, in its view, were represented by Catholicism (**33**). The history of these internal disagreements within the established Church proved to be a complicated and, at times, an intractable one, though the story was to undergo many shifts of emphasis and was to involve men holding a wide range of views between support for episcopacy on the one hand and rigid Presbyterianism on the other. The central area of disagreement was first articulated and mapped out in the early 1570s, as were the strategies to be adopted by the protagonists. The problem of the Puritans within the English Church had now been made a public one.

Part Three: Assessment

5 The Impact of the Reformation

The changes in church organisation and belief which have been described answered many of the points made by critics of the early sixteenth-century Church, but by 1570 the story was still far from complete. A Protestant regime had emerged after a generation of struggle between conservatives and reformers, but in the nation at large many people remained indifferent or lukewarm, if not opposed to the settlement. This variety of response was found among all sectors of society: the nobility and gentry, the clergy, the artisans and craftsmen in towns, and the farmers and peasants of the countryside. For the majority of the population it was not the diplomatic consequences of the break with Rome, nor the constitutional implications of the new relationship between Church and State that mattered. Their concerns were more direct: their parish churches and their guilds and fraternities; local shrines and religious houses; the liturgical year with its close associations with the agrarian calendar; and above all the provision of the sacramental 'rites of passage', from baptism through marriage and child-bearing to burial. On all these matters the changes between 1530 and 1570 had had a dramatic impact, and the sweeping nature of those changes must have disturbed people's confidence in the capacity of the Church to provide the one essential required of it, a secure and well-mapped path to salvation. Eventually that path came to be signposted not by the sacraments and intercessory prayers of Catholicism, but by the Bible and preaching of Protestantism. In 1570, however, a confusing mixture of signs existed, and the ultimate triumph of Protestantism could not easily be assumed. The progress of the Reformation varied from place to place, and its acceptance among different groups in society took place at different times. Out of this complex patchwork some broad geographical and social patterns can be discerned, and the story of Protestant evangelisation can be pieced together.

Geography

The long-held assumption of the division of the country into a religiously conservative and economically backward North and West and a Protestant and commercial South and East was based on the records of central government and was supported by the study of major rebellions such as the Pilgrimage of Grace. However, the growth of local studies of the Reformation over the last twenty-five years has challenged and refined that interpretation. Within relatively small areas, such as the counties of Kent, Norfolk and the West Riding, there were divisions between Catholic and Protestant deriving from a variety of causes, some economic, some political, and some concerned with local loyalties and factions (**29, 105, 106**). Most important of all in accounting for this diversity was the evangelistic effort of the preachers – men like Hugh Latimer, who was sent on a preaching campaign to Bristol in the 1530s and laid the foundations of a Protestant tradition in that western city which survived Marian persecution. In an age without any means of mass communication, when the revolutionary impact of the printing press had hardly penetrated beyond the intelligentsia, traditional lines of communication through the pulpit and through trade and marketing remained paramount.

In this context the southern and eastern counties were best placed to maintain contact with new ideas. Internally their proximity to the capital and the court, and to the universities, made access to Protestant preaching and literature easier for the gentry and clergy, as well as for some leading townsmen (**98**). Externally, the ports of the region had regular contact with the Protestant towns of northern Europe and such trading links no doubt eased the reception of Protestantism among the mercantile class in London, as well as among merchants' families in towns like Yarmouth and Faversham (**30, 86**, Clark). In addition, and among the farmers and artisans, the south-east had a number of localised groups of heretics or Lollards, who were likely to be attracted to Protestant evangelisation (**41**).

This evidence supports the generalisation and points to the early growth of Protestantism in the South and East. The evidence from the exiles and martyrs of Mary's reign adds further emphasis: about 40 per cent of the exiles under Mary came from London, Middlesex, Kent, Sussex, Essex, Suffolk, and Norfolk, and these same six counties accounted for three-quarters of the martyrs (**53, 7**). These figures, of course, refer only to the most zealous and committed Protestants. Important as they were for the future history of Protestantism, they only represent a tiny fraction of the population as a whole, and it would be wrong to assume that the south-east was wholeheartedly Protestant, even by 1570. The survival of Catholicism among the Sussex gentry has already been noted (see page 60), and recent work on Norfolk has shown that a county which was identified with an early and vigorous Protestant tradition also contained numerous and enduring pockets of Catholicism fortified by the influence of Thomas Howard, Duke of Norfolk (**105, 129**). Studies of the Kentish and Sussex ports have also shown how Protestant ideas polarised factions within those small communities (**29, 134**).

If Catholicism could survive in the South and East, could not Protestantism penetrate the North and West? The pioneering work of A. G. Dickens has shown early signs of Protestantism in Yorkshire communities as diverse as the scattered upland settlements around Halifax and the busy port of Hull (**43**). In south Lancashire the early reception of Protestant ideas was due to the contacts which a group of farmers, linked to the family of John Bradford of Manchester, had made whilst at Cambridge (**53**). In the West Country the preaching of Hugh Latimer has been noted; less well-known is the work of Matthew Price and a group of friends who disseminated Protestant ideas in the rural parishes of the Severn Valley during Henry VIII's reign (**135**).

So the broad pattern of Protestant evangelisation remains true, but with important qualifications. Firstly, the fragmentary nature of the evidence prevents us assuming speedy success with the mass of the population. Secondly, the sources do not provide any support for a simple socio-economic explanation of the pattern. And thirdly, we have plenty of evidence to show that at various levels, be they county, town or village, there were communities whose inhabitants did not share the religious views prevailing in their locality, whilst within some communities the arrival of Protestant ideas divided family and friends.

The parish clergy

Inevitably, when the pulpit was the chief means of communication, the spread of Protestantism was going to depend in large measure on the clergy. The earlier chapters have shown how Protestant divines, mostly educated at Cambridge, came to provide intellectual and administrative leadership for the Church, but the contribution of the parochial clergy requires assessment. The criticisms in Colet's sermon [**doc. 1**] suggest that the parochial clergy were not equipped for evangelising their congregations; and many, like Geoffrey Meredith of Upton in 1558, were happy to remain ignorant of royal Injunctions and Convocation articles whilst at the same time conscientiously carrying out their pastoral obligations of hearing confessions and teaching parishioners the *Pater Noster* (The Lord's Prayer). The dissolutions of the monasteries and chantries demoralised a profession, the nature of whose calling was being radically altered (**89**, O'Day, **143**). Despite this, it would be wrong to assume that no initiatives were being taken in the parishes. A former friar, Stephen Wilson, introduced Protestant ideas into the neighbourhood of Northampton in the 1530s, taking discussion of such matters as the real presence to the laity not only in the pulpit, but also in the pub—'The Sign of the Bell' in Northampton (**25**). There were others like Wilson, but their influence was essentially local and piecemeal, though in many cases it was also to be an enduring one. The only issue on which we can judge the parochial clergy in a wider context concerns clerical marriage, an issue related to but not necessarily linked to Protestantism. There is no doubt that large numbers of clergy followed the lead of Protestant bishops like Hooper, Cranmer and Ridley, and took wives during the reign of Edward VI. Whether these men married, as did Archbishop Holgate, to demonstrate their Protestantism, or whether they simply regularised a previously illegal arrangement cannot be known for certain. What can be said, however, is that some 2,000 were prosecuted under Mary, and that their geographical distribution is very similar to the patterns noticed among the exiles and martyrs of that reign (**89**, O'Day). The parish clergy, with few notable exceptions, went along fairly passively with the Reformation and, in that respect, may have been less influential than some sectors of the laity.

The gentry

The gentry, through their role in Parliament, were both the legislators of the changes and the instruments of the Marian reaction. In all of this they shared responsibility with the peers and the bishops who made up the House of Lords. In this respect then, as Thomas Cromwell recognised, the role of the gentry in Parliament was crucial to many stages of the process of reform, but Parliament was not the only arena for gentry influence. These men were the leaders of local society in their counties; through attendance at university, the Inns of Court, Parliament and the royal household, many of them acquired a breadth of experience and a range of contacts beyond the rest of the population. They were therefore not only the chief instruments of local government, but also the sector of society most likely to be aware of developments outside their own neighbourhoods and counties (**83**).

The changes of the 1530s greatly increased the standing of some gentry families in their localities. The purchase of former monastic lands helped to secure the economic fortunes of families such as the Spencers and the Cecils, and with those lands came opportunities for patronage within the Church, and a vested interest in the Reformation (**50, 99**). Such factors were important in identifying the gentry with the changes of the 1530s and 1540s, but did not necessarily make them Protestants. Contacts with Protestantism, when they arose, came not from legislation, but from attendance at university and at London. At university they made contact with humanist critics of the Church like John Redman, first Master of Trinity College, Cambridge, and John Cheke, whose influence at St John's College in Cambridge produced men, like William Cecil, who were ultimately to establish the Elizabethan governmental machine (**65**). At London, as students of the Inns of Court or while attending Parliament or court, the gentry would hear preachers, organised at St Paul's Cross by Cromwell, who defended and expounded government policy during the 1530s and, in Edward's reign, Protestants of the calibre of Hugh Latimer and Thomas Sampson (**81**). It was the twin influences of Cambridge and London which turned a civil servant, John Bradford, into a forceful Protestant preacher in Edward's reign (**55**).

Before 1558 the number of Protestant gentry remained small, even when they had powerful noble support from the Seymour and Dudley families in Edward's reign. In no part of the country, except perhaps in Kent where the influence of Thomas Cromwell was important, could it be said that a distinctive Protestant party of any size emerged in local politics among the gentry (**29, 46**). For the future, however, Protestant teachers and preachers in Cambridge and London had introduced reformed ideas to the next generation of politicians. In this way foundations were laid among the gentry, the most important political group in the nation, which, though they had to be covered over quickly during Mary's reign, were to prove sufficiently solid and permanent to sustain the

Elizabethan regime, and to enable it to carry out its policies in their own localities.

Towns

Contemporaries like Thomas Cromwell saw the importance of towns in spreading reformation ideas. Earlier this century the historian R. H. Tawney developed this idea, writing that 'the true English Reformation' took place among 'the trading classes of the towns, and of those rural districts which had been partially industrialized by the decentralization of the textile and iron industries' (**107**). Most towns were small – London being by far the largest, with about 40,000 people – and were chiefly concerned with marketing for their agricultural hinterland. The opportunities for corporations and townsmen to profit from the dissolved monasteries and chantries was welcome to communities which had been in economic decline; but these changes also brought disadvantages in the abolition of religious guilds which had played such a prominent part in late medieval civic life through mystery plays, processions and the like (**30**). Their abolition created a social and religious vacuum in larger towns like York and Coventry (**94, 18**), and a political one too in places like Lichfield where the guild of Our Lady and St John the Baptist was in effect the town council, since the town had no charter (**128**).

The effect of the Reformation on these communities was mixed and its progress far from uniform. Government policy brought Protestant preaching to Bristol in the 1530s (**46**) at about the same time that trading links introduced reformed ideas to Rye and Hull (**134, 43**); faction in Gloucester council was focussed on the preaching of parish priests in the 1540s (**30**); and a tradition of heresy in the small town of Cranbrook led to the early appearance of Protestantism there (**34**). In the reign of Edward VI a few towns, like Ipswich, even paid for a civic preacher to give four sermons a year (**30**), and under Mary places like Boston and Colchester provided support for Protestants (**132**) [**doc. 20**]. On the other hand, the dissolution of the monasteries resulted in riots at Exeter (**141**); York and Lichfield sought to retain their traditional guilds after 1547 (**94, 128**); and pastoral provision in places like Eccles [**doc. 14**] and Chipping Campden was reduced by the removal of chantry priests. The towns, therefore, as the natural centres for the exchange of ideas as well as of goods, played an important part in the Reformation, but their experiences do not establish a natural link between Protestant ideas and a nascent 'bourgeois capitalism'.

Everything of course, was written much larger in London. It is only to be expected that in the capital religious divisions would appear early among the leading citizenry. What was exceptional about London was the extent to which Protestantism gained support from members of the wider community, be they the apprentices who barracked conservative clergy in the 1530s (**121**) or the members of the underground churches which endured in Mary's reign, like those who attended that meeting in Plumbers Hall (**132**). Of course, the greater availability of Protestant preaching, at St Paul's Cross and elsewhere, contributed to the growth of Protestantism in London, but this was further advanced during Edward's reign when the city became the home of Protestant refugees fleeing from Catholic authorities on the Continent. Foreigners had always been part of London life, and in fact in 1535 fourteen Dutch Anabaptists had been burned as heretics by the government. After 1547, however, Protestant refugees were welcomed, though their radical congregational form of Calvinist church government, involving elected clergy and elders, caused some concern even to staunch Protestants such as Bishop Nicholas Ridley. The most famous of these congregations was that led by John à Lasco, but there were others elsewhere in the capital like that at Austin Friars where French, German, and Italian refugees organised themselves into one church. These groups of foreigners – and by the end of the reign similar groups had settled in Colchester, Southampton and Canterbury – acted as witnesses of reformed churchmanship to those rank and file townsmen with whom they came in contact (**42**).

The people

The most recent study of the Reformation maintains that 'on the whole, English men and women did not want the Reformation and most of them were slow to accept it when it came' (**103**). It is possible to accept the last part of this statement whilst at the same time admitting that in some areas Protestant views took an early hold on the people. This was particularly true, in the early years, in old centres of heresy like Bocking in Essex or the Chiltern hills (**92, 41**). Beyond these isolated cases the evidence is more sketchy and can be best approached by two methods. The most traditional is to look at the survival of Protestantism under Mary. The other and more recent method employed is the analysis of religious statements and bequests in the wills of the laity in this period.

The evidence from wills is vast and difficult to assess statistically, but some general comments can be made. For example, it was a persistent and important feature of medieval piety to provide for prayers for the dead, and this was commonly, though by no means exclusively, done by will [**doc. 13**]. The pioneering research of W. K. Jordan revealed that in his sample of counties the practice of making such endowments by will had declined in Hampshire and Buckinghamshire by the 1530s, but continued to have a firm hold on the laity of Somerset, Lancashire, Yorkshire and, surprisingly, of Kent and Norfolk also (**71**). His study shows that orthodox late medieval piety could be replaced quickly by Protestant commitment in some areas. As well as making specific bequests, testators usually dedicated the care of their soul; and the manner in which they made these dedications, whether through the traditional invocation to Our Lady and the saints or by a new formulation stressing the importance of faith and of Christ's sacrifice, can be a valuable index of religious change. Evidence from Londoners' wills for the period 1537 to 1547 suggests that veneration of Our Lady and the saints was in decline. This is also revealed by work on wills from Canterbury, on wills from the south-west, and even in Nottingham and Yorkshire samples from this date, where 22 per cent of will-makers omit references to Our Lady (**29, 43, 142**). These figures contrast greatly with the evidence from the city of York itself where almost all will-makers followed the traditional pattern (**94**). This evidence, however much it can suggest a decline in the hold of traditional beliefs, cannot, at this date, give statistical support for a general advance in Protestant belief. Nevertheless, it can point to pockets of Protestant support, such as in Thornbury in Gloucestershire or in eastern Northamptonshire where small groups of parishioners left statements of Protestant belief in their wills (**136, 104**) [**doc. 13**].

If we turn to the survival of Protestant groupings in Mary's reign, we see similar small gatherings of devotees but, among these, we also see evidence of links with each other, and also with the leadership of continental Protestantism. This was particularly true of a London group to which John Rough was pastor in 1557. This church provided financial support to imprisoned Protestants, was served as pastor for a time by the Swiss Augustine Bernher, and was suspected by the government of dangerous contact with the continental churches. The London group was exceptional in both its permanence and its level of organisation; most others had a fitful existence and depended on lay as opposed to clerical initiative. Typical of these laymen were Ralph Allerton of Great Bentley in Essex, who kept his congregation going despite living for a while 'in woods, barns, and other solitary places', and the London merchant Anthony Hickman, who shared meals accompanied by Bible-reading with fellow Protestants whilst 'keeping the doores shut for feare' (**132**). The links between these groups and the ministers were maintained by the safe houses provided by the laymen, or by conventional trade channels. Thus at Colchester three Edwardian pastors used the King's Head Inn as a base for ministries to congregations in London and elsewhere, whilst in an unnamed inn in the same town debates took place between orthodox Protestants and radical sectaries in 1555. Clearly London and Colchester were the main organising centres of this underground activity [**doc. 20**], but congregations could be found at Ipswich, and in remoter places such as South Molton in Devon and Shakerly in Lancashire, where night meetings were organised by a local layman whenever he could find an itinerant Protestant preacher (**132**).

Scattered though this evidence is, it is enough to show that 'the people' also made a contribution to the growth of Protestantism, but that growth was not inconsistent with the fact that these changes made little impact on the great majority of the population. It has been said that though few people avoided the rites of baptism, matrimony and burial, there is much evidence to suggest that, in this period, many of the poorer people never became regular church-goers and that most had only the scantiest understanding of religious doctrine (**108**). Statistics in this area are impossible to find and the subject is one which needs cautious treatment, but this state of affairs has to be acknowledged if the picture is to be complete. It was after all one of the chief claims of Protestants that they sought to overcome the ignorance of the people, and a regular complaint of those who did not share their zeal was that 'it was never merry England since we were impressed [forced] to come to church' (**104**).

The evidence suggests that there was a decline in the strength of conservative piety among the better-off elements in local communities; that there was positive advance of Protestant ideas among small groups in a few places; and that there was a good deal of ignorance and indifference among the poorer sort.

Occasionally the poorer sort would be encouraged, as in 1536 and 1569, to engage in open defiance of the Crown in defence of traditional religion, especially when that cause could be linked to other secular grievances (**51**). For the most part, however, opposition to the changes was localised and passive, not challenging authority. Sometimes this opposition was due to a powerful regional figure, like John Longland, Bishop of Lincoln, who, at his death in 1547, left a diocese with priests and laity as conservative as he was. Wills of the area show a strong tradition of belief in prayers for the dead, and Protestants were pursued and prosecuted quickly. He controlled preaching, and held regular visitations in the diocese, which covered nine counties before 1540, and stood in the tradition of Catholic reformers. He saw the faults in the existing Church, but sought reform from within. In this way he strove to retain the best of the old in this large area of England, and the best of the old was prayer. On leaving money to the almsmen of Henley in his will, he required them to say each morning five Our Fathers, five Hail Marys, and one Creed 'in the worship of the five wounds' (the five wounds were a popular source of piety and one seized on by the Pilgrimage of Grace). This was traditional piety, and Longland's role as he saw it was to preserve as much of it as possible (**25**). Just as Protestant bishops like Ridley and Hooper could, by example, give impetus to Protestant reform in Edward's reign, so conservative and conscientious men like Longland or Tunstall in Durham could help to retain attachment to the Catholic tradition among the people of their dioceses (**25, 131**).

In the years following 1559 this conservative tradition was maintained in many places by the Marian clergy who ministered to their parishioners and, as in Sussex, received support from sympathetic gentlemen (**82, 127, 133**). But this sort of opposition, though slowing down the spread of Protestantism, no longer challenged its domination within the governing classes. By 1570 a Protestant regime had emerged and had won support from the governing groups in most parts of provincial England. The universities were beginning to produce a steady supply of preaching ministers wishing to take that preaching to the parishes. The dramatic theological and liturgical changes had been clothed in an outward form which stressed continuity and stability for many church-goers. This may have disappointed the radicals, but was important in winning over the lukewarm and the uncertain. In this respect we can agree that, despite much ignorance and indifference, most English men and women slowly came to accept and even to welcome the Reformation and those changes in religious practice and political life which resulted from it. Opposition remained, but after 1570 the energies of the Church were directed as much against radical Protestants as against conservative Catholics. That fact in itself is testimony to the achievement of the years between 1530 and 1570.

Part Four: Documents

The Dean of St Paul's criticises the Church, 1511

The humanist scholar John Colet criticised the involvement of churchmen in worldly affairs in a sermon preached before Convocation. The clergy resented his outspoken views and sought his prosecution. These extracts are typical of humanist disenchantment with the late medieval church.

Ye are come together today, fathers and right wise men, to enter council; in the which, what ye will do and what matters ye will handle, yet we understand not. But we wish that once, remembering your name and profession, ye would mind the reformation of the Church's matter. For it was never more need, and the state of the Church did never desire more your endeavours . . .

To exhort you, reverend fathers, to the endeavour of reformation of the Church's estate, (because that nothing hath so disfigured the face of the Church as hath the fashion of secular and worldly living in clerks and priests) . . . Wherefore Saint Paul said chiefly unto priests and bishops: *Be you not conformable to this world, but be ye reformed.*

And first for to speak of pride of life: how much greediness and appetite of honour and dignity is nowadays in men of the Church? How run they, yea, almost out of breath, from one benefice to another; from the less to the more, from the lower to the higher? . . . Moreover . . . the most part of them doth go with so stately a countenance and with so high looks, that they seem not to be put in the humble bishopric of Christ, but rather in the high lordship and power of the world . . .

The second secular evil is carnal concupiscence. Hath not this vice grown and waxen in the Church as a flood of their lust, so that there is nothing looked for more diligently in this most busy time of the most part of priests than that that doth delight and please the senses? . . .

Covetousness is the third secular evil . . . O covetousness! of thee cometh these chargeful visitations of bishops. Of thee cometh the corruptness of courts, and these daily new inventions wherewith the silly people are so vexed . . .

The fourth secular evil that spotteth and maketh ill-favoured the face of the Church is the continual secular occupation, wherein priests and bishops nowadays doth busy themselves, the servants rather of men than of God; the warriors rather of this world than of Christ . . .

Lupton, J. H., *Life of Colet*, London, 1887, pp. 293–9.

document 2
The effect of Wycliffite writings, 1528

Thomas Topley, a Suffolk friar, was introduced to Wyclif's writings by Richard Foxe, curate of Steeple Bumpstead, and this, in conjunction with the preaching of Miles Coverdale, led him to hold an unorthodox opinion on the Eucharist.

It fortuned thus, about half a year ago, that the said sir Richard went forth, and desired me to serve his cure for him; and as I was in his chamber, I found a certain book called *Wickliff's Wicket*, whereby I felt in my conscience a great wavering for the time that I did read upon it, and afterwards, also, when I remembered it, it wounded my conscience very sore. Nevertheless, I consented not to it, until I had heard him preach, and that was upon St Anthony's day. Yet my mind was still much troubled with the said book (which did make the sacrament of Christ's body, in form of bread, but a remembrance of Christ's passion), till I heard sir Miles Coverdale preach, and then my mind was sore withdrawn from that blessed sacrament, insomuch that I took it then but for the remembrance of Christ's body.

Printed in (**19**), p. 232.

document 3
A layman attacks clerical wealth, 1528

Simon Fish wrote his satire A Supplication for the Beggars *whilst living abroad. This tract, which complained of the economic oppression of the laity by the clergy, was popular and had wide circulation on the eve of the Reformation Parliament.*

Here, if it please your grace to mark, ye shall see a thing far out of joint. There are within your realm of England 52 thousand parish churches. And this standing, that there be but ten households in every parish, yet are there five hundred thousand and twenty thousand households. And of every of these households hath every of the five orders of friars a penny a quarter for every order, that is for all the five orders, five pence a quarter for every house ... Oh! grievous and painful exactions thus yearly to be paid! from the which the people of your noble predecessors, the kings of the ancient Britons, ever stood free. And this they will have, or else they will procure him that will not give it them to be taken as an heretic ...

And what do all these greedy sort of sturdy, idle, holy thieves, with these yearly exactions that they take of the people? Truly, nothing but exempt themselves from the obedience of your grace. Nothing but translate all rule, power, lordship, authority, obedience and dignity from your grace unto them. Nothing but that all your subjects should fall into disobedience and rebellion against your grace and be under them.

Simon Fish, *A Supplication for the Beggars*, as printed in (**17**), pp. 670–1.

document 4
Thomas More is asked to answer the heretics, 1528

More was very concerned about the growth of heresy and thought Fish's book a dangerous pamphlet. The Bishop of London gave him a licence to keep such books so that he could defend the Church in his writings, particularly against the views expressed by William Tyndale.

Cuthbert, by divine permission bishop of London, to the very reverend and distinguished Sir Thomas More, his very dear brother and friend, greetings in the Lord and blessing.

Since of late, after the Church of God throughout Germany has been infested with heretics, there have been some sons of iniquity who are trying to introduce into this country of ours the old and accursed Wycliffite heresy and its foster-child the Lutheran heresy, by translating into our mother tongue some of the most subversive of their pamphlets, and printing them in great quantity. They are, indeed, striving with all their might to defile and infect this country with these pestilential doctrines, which are most repugnant to the truth of the Catholic faith ...

And since you, dearest brother, are distinguished as a second Demosthenes in our native language as well as in Latin, and you are in the habit of championing Catholic truth most keenly in every discussion, you cannot better occupy your spare time (if you can steal any from your duties) than in publishing something in English which will reveal to simple and uneducated men the crafty wickedness of the heretics, and will better equip such folk against such impious supplanters of the Church. In so doing you have a very distinguished example, that of our most illustrious lord, King Henry VIII, who stood up in defence of the sacraments of the Church against Luther, when he was doing all he could to undermine them, and thus win for himself for all time the immortal title of Defender of the Church ...

Go forth boldly, then, to such holy work, by which you will both benefit the Church of God and lay up for yourself an immortal name, and eternal glory in heaven. We beseech you in God's name so to do, strengthening the Church of God with your support. And to that end we give and grant you facilities and licence to keep and read books of this kind.

Given on the 7th. day of March 1528 and in the sixth year of our consecration.

Printed in (**17**), pp. 828–9.

document 5
Tyndale attacks pilgrimages, 1531

In his Answer to More *of 1531, Tyndale attacked many of the 'idolatrous' practices of traditional religion and defended his translation of the New Testament with its Lutheran implications.*

Pilgrimages.
To speak of pilgrimages, I say that a Christian man, so that he leave nothing undone at home that he is bound to do, is free to go whither he will; only after the doctrine of the Lord, whose servant he is, and not his own. If he go and visit the poor, the sick, and the prisoner, it is well done, and a work that God commandeth. If he go to this or that place to hear a sermon, or because his mind is not quiet at home; or if, because his heart is too much

occupied on his worldly businesses, by the reasons of occasions at home, he get him into a more quiet and still place, where his mind is more abstract, and pulled from worldly thoughts, it is well done. And in all these places, if whatsoever it be, whether lively preaching, ceremony, relic, or image stir up his heart to God, and preach the word of God, and the ensample of our Saviour Jesus, more in one place than in another, that he thither go, I am content.

But to believe that God will be sought more in one place than in another, or that God will hear thee more in one place than in another, or more where the image is than where it is not is a false faith, and idolatry, or image-service. For first, God dwelleth not in temples made with hands . . . Moreover, God in his testament bindeth himself unto no place . . . He setteth neither place nor time; but wheresoever and whensoever; so that the prayer of Job upon the dunghill was as good as Paul's in the temple.

Walter, H. (ed.), *An Answer to Sir Thomas More's Dialogues . . . by William Tyndale*, Parker Society, 1850, pp. 63–4.

document 6

Catherine of Aragon divorced, 1533

Here is Thomas Cranmer's account of the final stages in the divorce proceedings against the Queen, following consultation with the universities and with Convocation. The Queen steadfastly refused to recognise the authority of the court.

And first, as touching the final determination and concluding of the matter of divorce between my lady Katherine and the king's grace, which said matter, after the convocation in that behalf had determined and agreed according to the former consent of the universities, it was thought convenient by the king and his learned counsel, that I should repair unto Dunstable, which is within four miles unto Ampthill, where the said Katherine keepeth her house, and there to call her before me to hear the final sentence in the said matter. Notwithstanding, she would not at all obey thereunto; for when she was by doctor Lee cited to appear by a day, she utterly refused the same, saying, that inasmuch as her cause was before the pope, she would have none other judge; and therefore would not take me for her judge.

Nevertheless the 8th. day of May, according to the said appointment, I came unto Dunstable, my lord of Lincoln being assistant unto me, and my lord of Winchester, doctor Bell, Dr. Claybrooke, Dr. Trygonnell, Dr. Hewis, Dr. Olyver, Dr. Brythen, Mr. Bedell, with divers others learned in the law, being counsellors in the law for the king's part: and so there at our coming kept a court for the appearance of the said lady Katherine, where were examined certain witness which testified that she was lawfully cited and called to appear, whom for fault of appearance was declared *contumax*; proceeding in the said cause against her *in poenam contumaciae*, as the process of the law thereunto belongeth; which continued fifteen days after our coming thither. And the morrow after Ascension-day I gave final sentence therein, how that it was indispensable for the pope to license any such marriages.

This done, and after our rejourneying home again, the king's highness prepared all things convenient for the coronation of the queen [Anne Boleyn].

Cox, J. E. (ed.), *The Miscellaneous Writings of Thomas Cranmer*, Parker Society, 1846, pp. 244–5.

document 7
The submission of the clergy, 1534

In the Supplication against the Ordinaries of 1532, Parliament had attacked the legislative independence of the Church from royal control. Threatened with prosecution under the Statute of Praemunire (see page 20), the clergy submitted. This was then given statutory force and the Crown was granted positive powers within the Church.

Where the King's humble and obedient subjects the clergy of this realm of England have not only acknowledged according to the truth that the Convocation of the same clergy is always, hath been, and ought to be assembled only by the King's writ, but also submitting themselves to the King's Majesty hath promised *in verbo Sacerdotii* that they will never from henceforth presume to attempt, allege, claim, or put in ure or enact, promulge or execute any new canons, constitutions, ordinance provincial, or other, or by whatsoever other name they shall be called in the Convocation, unless the King's most royal assent and licence may to them be had to make, promulge, and execute the same, and that his Majesty do give his most royal assent and authority in that behalf . . . Be it therefore now enacted by authority of this present Parliament, according to the said submission and petition of the said clergy, that they nor any of them from henceforth shall presume to attempt, allege, claim, or put in ure any constitutions or ordinances provincial or synodal, or any other canons, nor shall enact, promulge or execute any such canons, constitutions, or ordinance provincial, by whatsoever name or names they may be called, in their Convocations in time coming, which always shall be assembled by authority of the King's writ, unless the same clergy shall have the King's most royal assent and licence to make, promulge and execute such canons, constitutions and ordinances provincial or synodal; upon pain of every one of the said clergy doing contrary to this act and being thereof convict to suffer imprisonment and make fine at the King's will . . .

Statutes of the Realm, iii, pp. 460–1.

document 8

The Act of Supremacy, 1534

This was the central act in the process of breaking with Rome and placing the Crown as the chief authority within the English Church. It was repealed by Mary. When the supremacy was restored by Elizabeth, the royal title was changed to Supreme Governor.

Albeit the King's Majesty justly and rightfully is and oweth to be the supreme head of the Church of England, and so is recognized by the clergy of this realm in their Convocations; yet nevertheless for corroboration and confirmation thereof, and for increase of virtue in Christ's religion within this realm of England, and to repress and extirp all errors, heresies, and other enormities and abuses heretofore used in the same, Be it enacted . . . that the King our sovereign lord, his heirs and successors kings of this realm, shall be taken, accepted, and reputed the only supreme head in earth of the Church of England called *Anglicana Ecclesia*, and shall have and enjoy annexed and united to the imperial crown of this realm as well the title and style thereof, as all honours, dignities, pre-eminences, jurisdictions, privileges, authorities, immunities, profits, and commodities, to the said dignity of the supreme head of the same Church belonging and appertaining; And that our said sovereign lord, his heirs and successors kings of this realm, shall have full power and authority from time to time to visit, repress, redress, reform, order, correct, restrain and amend all such errors, heresies, abuses, offences, contempts, and enormities, whatsoever they be, which by any manner spiritual authority or jurisdiction ought or may lawfully be reformed, repressed, ordered, redressed, corrected, restrained, or amended, most to the pleasure of Almighty God, the increase of virtue in Christ's religion, and for the conservancy of the peace, unity and tranquillity of this realm: any usage, custom, foreign laws, foreign authority, prescription or any other thing or things to the contrary hereof notwithstanding.

Statutes of the Realm, iii, p. 492.

document 9
The monasteries surveyed and dissolved, 1536, 1539

Document (a) forms part of the royal visitation of Yorkshire monasteries which reported on their value and their foundation, as well as on any relics or devotions associated with them. Document (b) is a grant of ex-monastic lands to Sir Richard Rich who, as Chancellor of the Court of Augmentations, was well placed to profit from them.

(a)

Basedale – Superstition – there they had the Virgin's milk. Founder Sir Ralph Everes. Rents £18.

Meaux – Founder the King. Rents £98. Superstition – here singulum of S Bernard is sometimes lent for pregnant women.

Nunburnholme – Founder Lord Dakers. Rents £7. Here they have part of the Holy Cross.

North Ferriby – Founder the Earl of Cumberland. The house owes £80. Here St Gratianus is worshipped.

Haltemprice – Founder the Duke of Richmond. Rents £104. Here is a pilgrimage to Thomas Wake for fever and in veneration they have the arm of St George and part of the Holy Cross & the girdle of St Marie healthful for childbirth (as is thought).

Clay, J. W., *Yorkshire Monasteries, Suppression papers*, Yorkshire Archaeological Society, Record Series, 48, p. 16.

(b)

Sir Richard Ryche, Chancellor of the Court of Augmentations. Grant in fee of the manors of Magna Bursted, Westhouse, Whites, Gurneys, Bukwynes, Cowbridge and Chalwedon, Essex; the rectory and the advowson of the vicarage of Magna Bursted; and certain messuages, mills, lands, &c., in Magna Bursted, Parva Bursted, Billerica, Gyngmountey, Mountneysyng, Hoton, Stok, Buttesbury, Laynedon, Nevendon, Lachendon, Bastildon, and Langdon, Essex; which premises belonged to the late monastery of Stratford Langthorne, Essex; and all possessions of Stratford Langthorne in the above named places, in as full manner as Wm. Huddelston, the late abbot, held the same:– Also the great mansion or messuage now in the tenure of the said Richard within the close circuit, &c., of the late house of Augustine Friars, London, with a great hall, bakehouse, stable, &c., and certain places thereto adjoining, i.e. the messuage or tenement with garden, in which Wm. Shirlande now dwells, all those chambers and houses late in the tenure of Richard Duke, an enclosure and land called "le Cloyster", the kitchen of the said late Friars near the said Cloyster, a curtilage and well therein between the said cloister and the said tenement of Wm. Shirlande, and the house situated on the South side of the said curtilage; To hold by the annual rent of £10. with liberties.

(**1**), xiv (part 1), no. 1354.

document 10

Hugh Latimer preaches before Convocation, 1536

Latimer was one of the leading reformist preachers and had been made Bishop of Worcester in 1535. The choice of him to preach the Convocation sermon marked an important advance for the Protestants at this time. However, when the Act of Six Articles restored conservative practices in 1539, Latimer resigned his bishopric and he was later martyred under Mary. His sermon of 1536 recalls document 1.

Wherefore lift up your heads, brethren, and look about with your eyes, spy what things are to be reformed in this church of England. Is it so hard, is it so great a matter for you to see the many abuses in the clergy, many in the laity? . . . How think you by the ceremonies that are in England, oft-times, with no little offence of weak consciences, contemned; more oftener with superstition so defiled, and so depraved, that you may doubt whether it were better some of them to tarry still, or utterly to take them away? Have not our forefathers complained of the ceremonies, of the superstition, and estimation of them?

Do ye see nothing in our holidays? of the which very few were made at the first, and they to set forth goodness, virtue and honesty: but sithens, in some places, there is neither mean nor measure in making new holidays, as who should say this one thing is serving of God, to make this law, that no man may work. But what doth the people on these holidays? Do they give themselves to godliness, or else ungodliness? See ye nothing, brethren? If you see not, yet God seeth. God seeth all the whole holidays to be spent miserably in drunkenness, in glossing, in strife, in envy, in dancing, dicing, idleness, and gluttony. He seeth all this, and threateneth punishment for it. He seeth it, which neither is deceived in seeing, nor deceiveth when he threateneth.

Thus men serve the devil; for God is not thus served, albeit ye say ye serve God. No, the devil hath more service done unto him on one holiday, than on many working days.

Corrie, G. E. (ed.), *Sermons of Hugh Latimer* (Parker Society, 1845), pp. 52–3.

document 11
Cromwell's injunctions, 1536

These injunctions were promulgated under the authority of the King who had appointed Cromwell as Vicegerent in matters ecclesiastical. The clauses were directed at the pastoral responsibilities of the clergy and these extracts refer to teaching the laity the faith and to making the Bible available to them – a practice which the bishops later sought to restrict.

5. Also in the same their sermons, and other collations, the parsons, vicars and other curates aforesaid shall diligently admonish the fathers and mothers, masters and governors of youth, being under their care, to teach, or cause to be taught, their children and servants, even from their infancy, their *Pater Noster*, the Articles of our Faith, and the Ten Commandments, in their mother

tongue, and the same so taught, shall cause the said youth oft to repeat and understand. . .

7. *Item*, that every parson or proprietary of any parish church within this realm, shall on this side the feast of *S. Peter ad Vincula* next coming, provide a book of the whole Bible, both in Latin, and also in English, and lay the same in the choir, for every man that will to look and read thereon, and shall discourage no man from the reading of any part of the Bible, whether in Latin or in English; but rather comfort, exhort and admonish every man to read the same as the very word of God, and the spiritual food of man's soul, whereby they may the better know their duties to God, to their sovereign lord the King, and their neighbour: ever gently and charitably exhorting them that, using a sober and modest behaviour in the reading and inquisition of the true sense of the same, they do in no wise stiffly or eagerly contend or strive one with another about the same but refer the declaration of those places that be in controversy to the judgement of them that be better learned.

(**8**), vol. ii, pp. 6–9.

document 12

Heresy comes near the court, 1546

During the conservative reaction of Henry's later years, some distinguished Protestant clergy and some gentry fell foul of the authorities. Anne Askew, a Lincolnshire gentlewoman, had been on the fringes of Catherine Parr's circle whilst visiting London.

The eighteenth day of June, 1546, were arraigned at the Guild Hall, for heresy, Doctor Nicholas Shaxton, sometimes bishop of Salisbury, Nicholas White of London, gentleman; Anne Keme, alias Anne Askewe, gentlewoman, and wife of Thomas Keme, gentleman, of Lincolnshire; and John Hadlam, of Essex, tailor; and were this day first indicted of heresy and after arraigned on the same, and there confessed their heresies against the sacrament of the altar, without any trial of a jury and so had judgment to be burnt. . .

The morning after, being the nineteenth day of June, Doctor Shaxton and Nicholas White, by the good exhortation and doctrine of the bishops of London and Worcester and divers other doctors, these two persons were converted from their heresy of the sacrament of the altar unto the true belief of the said sacrament; but Anne Askewe, alias Keme, was had to the Tower of London and there set on the rack, where she was sore tormented, but she would not convert for all the pain. . .

The sixteenth of July was burnt in Smithfield John Lascelles, gent., Anne Keme, alias Askewe, gentlewoman, John Hemley, priest, and John Hadlam, tailor, which four persons were before condemned by the King's laws of heresy against the sacrament of the altar; . . . and by the King's commandment Doctor Shaxton, afore condemned as these persons were, preached there in Smithfield, declaring his error that he had been in of the said sacrament, and after his reconciliation had the King's pardon.

Wriothesley, C. *A Chronicle of England*, Camden Society, 1875–7, ii, pp. 167–70.

document 13

Lay declarations of belief, 1540 and 1548

Wills are a major source for assessing the beliefs of the laity. Document (a) has been chosen to illustrate the extent of traditional piety in 1540, and document (b) to show the early appearance of Protestantism in 1548. These documents are also of interest because the conservative will comes from London and the Protestant one from Halifax in Yorkshire. They are therefore atypical, but serve to warn us that diversity existed even within regions.

(a) The will of Joan Brytten of London, 1540

I Jone Brytten of the parrische off Saynt Michaels in Wodstrete, syke in my body, be quethe my sole unto Allmyghthy God and unto Owre Blessid Lady and unto all the holli company in hevon, and my body to be byrid within the parrische chyrche of Saynt Gregoris by Poles undur a stone ther preparid all redy for me. I be qyethe unto the hi awter of Saynt Michaels for mi tithes necligent forgotten 8*d*. I will have at the tyme of mi biriall halffe a trintall of massis 5*s*. 4*d*. I wyll have 6 pristes bysyd the parson, the clarke and the sexten and be quethe them for there labur 4*s*. 10*d*. I will have a fore nonis knill 20*d*. The peles 6*d*. I wyll have 5 llb tappres the prise 15*d*. and 5 childyrne to bear them 10*d*. and 200 pownd tapires and the childyrne to bere them by fore the crose 10*d*. I vill that 4*s*. be delid in obolos bred [shared in halfpenny bread] at the tyme off mi birriall, also I will that a dyner be made for them that be out in trust of mi wyll the day of mi byriall, the pris 3*s*. 4*d*. Also I will at my dethe a inveteri off mi plat and off all the rest off mi godis be made and so presid and sold and than when the charges off mi birring and mi be questes payd the rest off mi godis I wyll that a prist schall syngke for mi sole, mi master Milard sole, his wiffes sole and all Cristin soles with in the chirch off Saynt Gregores in London for one halffe ere, and in the cherche off Saynt Michaels in Wodestret for the space of one quarter off a ere or more yff the godes will exsetende. . .

Darlington, I., (ed.), *London Consistory Court Wills 1492–1547*, London Record Society, 1967, p. 69.

(b) The will of Edward Hoppaye of Halifax, 1548

I beleve that my Redemer lyveth, and that at the last daye I shall arise out of the erthe and in my flesche shall se my Saviour. This my hoope is laid up in my bosome unto the last daye, that I and all other faithfull shall appere bifore the maiestie seatte of God . . and towchyng the welthe of my saull, the faith that I have takyn and reherced is sufficient, as I beleve, without any other man's worke or workes. My beleve is that theire is but one God and one mediator betwixt God and man, which is Jesus Christe, so that I accepte non in hevyn, neither in erthe, to be my mediatour betwixt God and me, but he onlie . . . and towchyng the distribution of my goodes, my purpose is to bestowe them that they may bee accepted as the fructes of faithe, so that I do not suppose that my merite be by bestowyng of them, but my merite is faithe in Jesus Christe only, by which faithe suche workes ar good according to Christ wordes, Matthew 25, *I was hungre and thou did gyve me meate*, etc. And it folowithe, *that ye have done to the least of my brether, you have done it to me*. A good warke maketh not a good man, but a good man makith good workes. For a righteouse man lyveth by faithe. And thus I rest in conscience concernyng my faith. . . .

(**43**), p. 217.

document 14

Chantry priests are missed, 1566

In many large upland parishes the chantry priests helped to maintain the regular services of the Church for the scattered congregations. In these areas the Chantries Act of 1546 drastically reduced clerical manpower, and in parishes like Deane and Eccles the effects of this shortage were still being felt twenty years later.

Report of the Commission instituted by Letters Patent 12 June 1566 in the chancel of Eccles church formerly property of Whalley Abbey. Item – that the nomber of the persons inhabytinge within the parrishes of Eccles and Deane amount to six thowsand and five hundreth persons and that the said parrishes of Eccles dothe conteyn in length viii miles and in breadth five myles. And the said parrishe of Deane in length nine miles and in breadthe fyve miles at the least by theyre estymacion. Item that theare is nowe at the Churche of Eccles, one vicar and at the Churche of Deane one other Vycar whiche Vicar of Eccles receyveth for his stypend yearelye of the Quenes majesty the somme of £16 8s. 4d. whereof tenne poundes was lately graunted unto hym by the Quenes highnes that nowe is in augmentacion of his stypend which before was but twentie nobles. . . And the sayde Vycar of Deane hath yerelye of the Quene a stypend of foure pounds which foure pounds he had alwayes at the hands of the said Abbott and Covent of the saide late monasterye.

Item there was in tyme past, fowre Chauntry preestes daylie serveinge at the saide Churche of Eccles, which nowe lyve abrode at their pleasure, upon ther pencions and there was also three stypendarie Preestes, daylie serving at the said church every one of which receyved yerelie for their wages, the somme of fyve pounds, over and beside one preeste which served at a certyne chappell called Ellynebrook within the saide parrishe of Eccles, which lyved uppon the devocion of suche as used to repayre thither, to hear devyne servyce, and there was also at the parrishe Churche of Dean, three stypendarie priestes that dailye served there over and besides twoo priestes that served at two chappells within the saide parrishe of Dean, called Halghton chappell and Horwiche chappell and had no wages but upon Devocion as is aforeseyd, but what wages the stipendarie priests servinge at Deane aforesaide receyved or had yerely, they knowe not . . . that there is nowe but two priests to serve the seyd cure of all the sayed parrishe, that is to saye one priest commonlye called the Vicar of Eccles and the other commonly called the Vicar of Deane.

Bretton Hall MSS. BEA/C3/B33 No. 66.

The communion service, 1549, 1552, 1559

These extracts from the Book of Common Prayer *show how the doctrine of the Eucharist changed in the three Acts of Uniformity.*

(a) 1549

Graunt us therefore (gracious lorde) so to eate the fleshe of thy dere sonne Jesus Christ, and to drynke his bloud in these holy Misteries, that we may continuallye dwell in hym, and he in us, that our synfull bodyes may bee made cleane by his body, and our soules washed through hys most precious bloud. Amen. . .
And when he delivereth the Sacrament of the body of Christe, he shall say to every one these woordes.

The body of our Lorde Jesus Christe whiche was geuen for thee, preserue thy bodye and soule unto euerlasting lyfe.

And the Minister deliuering the Sacrament of the bloud, and geuing every one to drinke once and no more, shall say,

The bloud of our Lorde Jesus Christe which was shed for thee, preserue thy bodye and soule unto euerlastyng lyfe.

(b) 1552

Then the Priest standing up shall saye, as foloweth.

Almighty God oure heauenly father, whiche of thy tender mercye dyddest geue thine onely Sonne Jesus Christ, to suffre death upon the crosse for our redempcion, who made there (by hys one oblacion of hymselfe once offered) a full, perfecte, and sufficiente sacrifice, oblacion, and satisfaccion, for the synnes of the whole worlde, and dyd institute, and in hys holye Gospell commaund us to continue, a perpetuall memorye of that his precious death, untyll hys comynge agayne: Heare us O mercyefull father wee beseeche thee; and graunt that wee, receyuing these thy creatures of bread and wyne, accordinge to thy sonne our Sauioure Jesus Christ's holy institution, in remembraunce of his death and passion, maye be partakers of his most blessed body and bloud: . . .

And when He delyuereth the bread, he shall saye.

Take and eate this, in remembraunce that Christe dyed for thee, and feede on him in thy hearte by faythe, with thankesgeuing.

And the Minister that delyuereth the cup, shal saye.

Drinke this in remembraunce that Christ's bloude was shed for thee, and be thankefull.

The First and Second Prayer Books of Edward VI, Everyman edn., 1910, pp. 225, 589.

(c) 1559 (The prayer before Communion was the same as that of 1552.)

The body of our Lord Jesus Christ which was given for thee, preserve thy body and soul into everlasting life: and take and eat this in remembrance that Christ died for thee, and feed on him in thine heart by faith, with thanksgiving.

And the minister that delivereth the cup, shall say,

The blood of our Lord Jesus Christ, which was shed for thee, preserve thy body and soul unto everlasting life: and drink this in remembrance that Christ's blood was shed for thee, and be thankful.

Clay, W. K. (ed.), *Liturgies and Occasional Forms of Prayer . . . Queen Elizabeth*, Parker Society, 1851, p. 195.

document 16

Married priests, 1549, 1559

Clerical marriage was often an important public statement for Protestant clergy. An Act of 1549 legalised such marriages, although celibacy was still the ideal. The Injunctions of 1559 restored clerical marriage but the terms set out show the conservative attitude of the Queen on this issue.

(a) 1549

Although it were not only better for the estimation of priests, and other ministers in the Church of God, to live chaste, sole, and separate from the company of women and the bond of marriage, but also thereby they might the better intend to the administration of the gospel, and be less intricated and troubled with the charge of household . . . and that it were most to be wished that they would willingly and of their selves endeavour themselves to a perpetual chastity and abstinence from the use of women:

Yet forasmuch as the contrary has rather been seen, and such uncleanness of living, and other great inconveniences, not meet to be rehearsed, have followed of compelled chastity, and of such laws as have prohibited those (such persons) the godly use of marriage; it were better and rather to be suffered in the commonwealth, that those which could not contain, should, after the counsel of Scripture, live in holy marriage, than feignedly abuse with worse enormity outward chastity or single life.

Statutes of the Realm, iv, part i, p. 67.

(b) 1559

XXIX. Item, although there be no prohibition by the word of God, nor any example of the primitive Church, but that the priests and ministers of the Church may lawfully, for the avoiding of fornication, have an honest and sober wife, and that for the same purpose the same was by Act of Parliament in the time of our dear brother King Edward VI made lawful, whereupon a great number of the clergy of this realm were then married, and so yet continue; yet because there hath grown offence, and some slander to the Church by lack of discreet and sober behaviour in many ministers of the Church, both in choosing of their wives and indiscreet living with them, the remedy whereof is necessary to be sought: it is thought, therefore very necessary that no manner of priest or deacon shall hereafter take to his wife any manner of woman without the advice and allowance first had upon good examination by the bishop of the same diocese, and two justices of the peace of the same shire . . .

(**9**), p. 431.

document 17
Reforming bishops, 1552

Hooper's visitation injunctions to the clergy of the diocese of Gloucester set out clearly the main tenets of the Protestant faith as established in Edward's reign while at the same time warning against the more extreme forms of new religious ideas. They are typical of the injunctions of other Protestant bishops.

6. *Item*, that the doctrine of the Anabaptists, denying the christening of infants, and affirming the rebaptizing and christening again of those which were before baptized in their infancy, as also affirming all manner of goods and chattel to be in common (saving such as are contained in the law of charity), and that all authority of magistrates should be removed from the church of God, and

such other like doctrines, and their sects, are very pernicious and damnable.

7. *Item*, that they and every of them do diligently teach and preach the justification of man to come only by the faith of Jesus Christ, and not by the merit of any man's good works; albeit that good works do necessarily follow justification, the which before justification are of no value or estimation before God. . .

9. *Item*, that the doctrine of the schoolmen of purgatory, pardons, prayers for them that are departed out of this world, the veneration, invocation, and worshipping of saints or images, is contrary and injurious to the honour of Christ our only Mediator and Redeemer. . .

10. *Item*, that in the sacrament of the Body and Blood of the Lord there is no transubstantiation of the bread and wine into the Body and Blood of Christ, or any manner of corporal or local presence of Christ in, under, or with the bread and wine, but spiritually by faith. . . So we receive the confirmation and augmentation of all the merits and deservings of Christ.

(**8**), pp. 269–70.

document 18

Caution advised, 1554

Stephen Gardiner, Bishop of Winchester, had been the leader of the conservatives in the reign of Henry VIII and had been imprisoned in Edward's reign. Pleased at the restoration of Catholicism, he nevertheless advised Cardinal Pole to proceed cautiously with the return of the papacy and in particular to guarantee the titles of owners of former monastic estates.

After my most hearty commendations: I humbly thank your Most Reverend Lordship for your letters, in which you rejoice with me that I have returned to that state and condition which I have for a long time desired to recover and to achieve, in the hope of seeing, with the help of God, the rest of the realm restored to the same unity, through which we shall be able all with one voice to glorify God the Father through Jesus Christ. To which end an illustrious legation has been entrusted to you, which I do not doubt you will execute in such a manner that condescending to our infirmities, as already you have begun to do, you will proceed with such steps that, by contemning, as beneath your notice, the offence of some, others may be encouraged and induced by good means to desire that of which they should be desirous, without fearing the loss of those things which they would so unwillingly abandon.

For this purpose it would be well that it should please your illustrious Lordship to write to the Parliament now in session a letter which should treat, in general only, the question of unity in religion, with such moderation that the right of the pope would be rather suggested than be expressed in clear words, and even that not so precisely done that they could conclude it to be imminent. Such a letter would be a good occasion, provided that your Most Reverend Lordship on this occasion declared and made it known to the leaders of the people of this realm that in the reformation which we desire to effect in our native land there is no intention of making any alteration in the possessions and temporal inheritances throughout the realm. . . Which matter, so set forth and tempered with such good words as your wisdom will know how to use, together with the knowledge that you are able to perform such a promise, will have, as I think, such weight as will suffice to remove from the minds of men that great obstacle which alone, as many prudently fear, could hinder in the eyes of the people our holy purpose and intention. . .

With commendations to your illustrious Lordship and offers of my service, I pray God, etc. From my house in Southwark, 5 April, 1554.

> Your Most Illustrious Lordship's
> humble and daily orator,
> Stephen

Muller, J. A. (ed.), *The Letters of Stephen Gardiner*, Cambridge University Press, 1933, pp. 464–7.

document 19

The Heresy Acts revived, 1554

The following Act restored the medieval heresy laws and enabled the persecutions of Mary's reign to take place.

For the eschewing and avoiding of errors and heresies, which of late have risen, grown, and much increased within this realm, for that the ordinaries have wanted authority to proceed against those that were infected therewith: be it therefore ordained and enacted by authority of this present Parliament, that the statute made in the fifth year of the reign of King Richard II, concerning the arresting and apprehension of erroneous and heretical preachers, and one other statute made in the second year of the reign of King Henry IV, concerning the repressing of heresies and punishment of heretics, and also one other statute made in the second year of the reign of King Henry V, concerning the suppression of heresy and Lollardy, and every article, branch, and sentence contained in the same three several Acts, and every of them, shall from the twentieth day of January next coming be revived, and be in full force, strength, and effect to all intents, constructions, and purposes for ever.

Statutes of the Realm, iv, part i, p. 244.

document 20

A humble heretic martyred, 1557

George Eagles was executed in 1557 in Colchester. In this account of his sufferings, John Foxe showed the fortitude of the reformers and the divine wrath visited on their persecutors. His use of biblical parallels reinforced the message, and the account is a good example of the style of this influential work.

Among other Martyrs of singular vertue and constancy, one *George Eagles* deserveth not the least admiration, but is so much the more to be commended, for that he, having little learning or none, most manfully served and fought under the banner of Christs Church. . . . we ought to glorifie God the more thereby in his holiness, which in so blind a time inspired him with the gift of preaching, and constancy of suffering: who after a certain time he had used the occupation of a Taylour, being eloquent and of good utterance, gave and applied himself to the Profit of Christs Church. . .

Now when he had profited Christs Church in this sort, by going about and preaching the Gospel a year or two, and especially in *Colchester*, a..d the quarters thereabout . . . And albeit it was well known, that poor *Eagles* did never any thing seditiously against the Queen, yet to cloak an honest matter withal, and to cause him to be the more hated of the People, they turned Religion into a Civil offence and crime, and though he defended his cause stoutly and boldly, making a full declaration of his Religion, or Faith before the Judges: yet could he not bring it to pass by any means, but that he must needs be indicted (as is said) of Treason. . .

This thing done, he was carried to the New-Inn, called the sign of the *Crown* in *Chelmsford*, by the beastly *Bayliffs* which some of them were they that before did their best to take him. . .

With him were cast certain Thieves also, and the next day, when they were brought out to be executed with him, there happened a thing that did much set forth and declare the innocency and godlyness of this man. For being led between two Thieves to the place where he should suffer. . . Then one *William Swallow* of *Chelmsford* a Bayliff . . . did hackle off his head, and sometime hit his neck, and sometime his Chin, and did fowly mangle him, and so opened him. Notwithstanding this blessed Martyr of Christ abode stedfast and constant in the very midst of his torments. . .

His Head was set up at *Chelmsford* on the Market Cross on a long Pole, and there stood till the Wind did blow it down, and lying certain days in the street tumbled about, one caused it to be buried in the Church yard in the night. Also a wonderful work of God was it that he shewed on this wicked Bayliff *Swallow*, who within short space after this was so punished, that all the hair went well near off his head, his eyes were as it were closed up, and could scantly see, the nails of his fingers and toes went clean off.

(**7**), 1684 edn., iii, pp. 700–1.

document 21

The Act of Uniformity, 1559

This Act, with the Act of Supremacy, established the terms of the Elizabethan settlement. There were severe penalties on those clergy failing to comply with it and, in another clause, it imposed the famous 12d. fine on laity not attending church.

And further be it enacted by the queen's highness, with the assent of the Lords and Commons in this present Parliament assembled, and by authority of the same, that all and singular ministers in any cathedral or parish church, or other place within this realm of England, Wales, and the marches of the same, or other the queen's dominions, shall from and after the feast of the Nativity of St. John Baptist next coming be bounden to say and use the Matins, Evensong, celebration of the Lord's Supper and administration of each of the sacraments, and all their common and open prayer, in such order and form as is mentioned in the said book, so authorized by Parliament in the said fifth and sixth years of the reign of King Edward VI, with one alteration or addition of certain lessons to be used on every Sunday in the year, and the form of the Litany altered and corrected, and two sentences only added in the delivery of the sacrament to the communicants, and none other or otherwise.

And that if any manner of parson, vicar, or other whatsoever minister . . . refuse to use the said common prayers . . . in such order and form as they be mentioned . . ., [he] shall lose and forfeit to the queen's highness, her heirs and successors, for his first offence, the profit of all his spiritual benefices or promotions coming or arising in one whole year next after his conviction; and also that the person so convicted shall for the same offence suffer imprisonment by the space of six months, without bail or mainprize.

And if any such person once convicted of any offence concerning the premises, shall after his first conviction eftsoons offend, and be thereof, in form aforesaid, lawfully convicted, that then the same person shall for his second offence suffer imprisonment by the space of one whole year, and also shall therefore be deprived, *ipso facto*, of all his spiritual promotions.

And if any such persons or persons, after he shall be twice convicted in form aforesaid, shall offend against any of the premises the third time, . . . [he] shall be deprived, *ipso facto*, of all his spiritual promotions, and also shall suffer imprisonment during his life. . .

And that from and after the said feast of the Nativity of St. John Baptist next coming, all and every person and persons inhabiting within this realm, or any other the queen's majesty's dominions, shall diligently and faithfully, having no lawful or reasonable excuse to be absent, endeavour themselves to resort to their parish church or chapel accustomed, or upon reasonable let thereof, to some usual place where common prayer and such service of God shall be used in such time of let, upon every Sunday and other days ordained and used to be kept as holy days, and then and there to abide orderly and soberly during the time of the common prayer, preachings, or other service of God there to be used and ministered; upon pain of punishment by the censures of the Church, and also upon pain that every person so offending shall forfeit for every such offence twelve pence, to be levied by the churchwardens of the parish where such offence shall be done, to the use of the poor of the same parish, or the goods, lands, and tenements of such offender by way of distress.

Statutes of the Realm, iv, part i, pp. 355–8.

document 22

The defence of the settlement, 1562

John Jewel, Bishop of Salisbury, wrote An Apology of the Church of England *to defend the settlement against its international critics. In these extracts, he refers to the example of the martyrs, refutes the charge of schism, and challenges the claims of the papacy.*

But we truly, seeing that so many thousands of our brethren in these last twenty years have borne witness unto the truth in the midst of most painful torments that could be devised; and when princes, desirous to restrain the gospel, sought many ways, but prevailed nothing; and that now almost the whole world doth begin to open their eyes to behold the light; we take it that our cause hath already been sufficiently declared and defended, and think it not needful to make many words, since the very matter saith enough for itself. . .

We believe that there is one church of God, and that the same is not shut up (as in times past among the Jews) into some one corner or kingdom, but that it is catholic and universal, and dispersed throughout the whole world; so that there is now no nation which can truly complain that they be shut forth, and may not be one of the church and people of God; and that this church is the kingdom, the body, and the spouse of Christ; and that Christ alone is the prince of this kingdom; that Christ alone is the head of this body; and that Christ alone is the bridegroom of this spouse.

Furthermore, that there be divers degrees of ministers in the church; whereof some be deacons, some priests, some bishops; to whom is committed the office to instruct the people, and the whole charge and setting forth of religion. Yet notwithstanding we say that there neither is, nor can be any one man, which may have the whole superiority in this universal state; for that Christ is ever present to assist his church, and needeth not any man to supply his room, as his only heir to all his substance; and that there can be no one mortal creature, which is able to comprehend or

101

conceive in his mind the universal church, that is to wit, all the parts of the world, much less able to put them in order, and to govern them rightly and duly. . .

And that neither the pope, nor any other worldly creature, can no more be head of the whole church, or a bishop over all, than he can be the bridegroom, the light, the salvation, and life of the church: for these privileges and names belong only to Christ, and be properly and only fit for him alone. . .

And therefore, sithence the bishop of Rome will now-a-days so be called, and challengeth unto himself an authority that is none of his; besides that he doth plainly contrary to the ancient councils and contrary to the old fathers, we believe that he doth give unto himself, as it is written by his own companion Gregory, a presumptuous, a profane, a sacrilegious, and an antichristian name; that he is also the king of pride: that he is Lucifer, which preferreth himself before his brethren; that he hath forsaken the faith, and is the forerunner of antichrist.

Booty, J. E. (ed.), *An Apology of the Church of England by John Jewel*, Cornell University Press, 1963, pp. 14, 24–6.

The Reformation vindicated, 1563

The title page of the first English edition of Foxe's Book of Martyrs *(opposite), as it later came to be called, shows how the Protestants, on the left, served God through suffering and preaching while the Catholics, on the right, were lost in idolatry. This pictorial representation of the two faiths was to be a powerful image of the Reformation for many generations of Protestants.*

tyranny of
Catholics

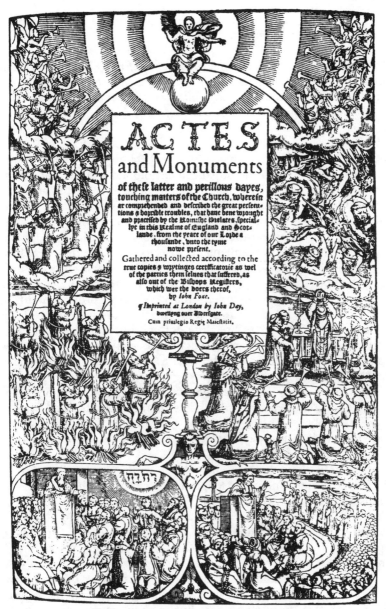

(**7**), 1563, title page.

document 24
Enforcing the vestments, 1566

These orders, or Advertisements, *requiring conformity in ceremonies were issued by Archbishop Parker. Their legal status was uncertain as he had failed to get the assent of the Queen, although it was a letter from her which had initiated the move towards greater conformity.*

The Preface
The queen's majesty, of her godly zeal, calling to remembrance how necessary it is to the advancement of God's glory, and to the establishment of Christ's pure religion for all her loving subjects, especially the state ecclesiastical, to be knit together in one perfect unity of doctrine, and to be conjoined in one uniformity of rites and manners in the ministration of God's holy word, in open prayer and ministration of sacraments, as also to be of one decent behaviour in their outward apparel . . . hath by her letters directed unto the Archbishop of Canterbury and metropolitan, required, enjoined, and straitly charged, that . . . some orders might be taken, whereby all diversities and varieties among them of the clergy and the people (as breeding nothing but contention, offence, and breach of common charity, and be against the laws, good usage, and ordinances of the realm) might be reformed and repressed. . .

Item, that every minister saying any public prayers, or ministering the sacraments or other rites of the Church, shall wear a comely surplice with sleeves, to be provided at the charges of the parish; and that the parish provide a decent table standing on a frame for the Communion Table.

Item, that they shall decently cover with carpet, silk, or other decent covering, and with a fair linen cloth (at the time of the ministration) the Communion Table, and to set the Ten Commandments upon the east wall over the said table.

Item, that all communicants do receive kneeling, and as is appointed by the laws of the realm and the queen's majesty's Injunctions. . .

Item, that they and all ecclesiastical persons or other, having any ecclesiastical living, do wear the cap appointed by the Injunctions. And they to wear no hats but in their journeying.

Item, that they in their journeying do wear their cloaks with sleeves put on, and like in fashion to their gowns, without guards, welts, or cuts.

Item, that in their private houses and studies they use their own liberty of comely apparel.

Item, that all inferior ecclesiastical persons shall wear long gowns of the fashion aforesaid, and caps as afore is prescribed.

Item, that all poor parsons, vicars, and curates do endeavour themselves to conform their apparel in like sort so soon and as conveniently as their ability will serve to the same.

(**9**), pp. 467, 470–1, 474.

document 25

A Puritan congregation in London, 1567

Members of the Plumbers Hall congregation were summoned before Bishop Grindal. Their replies show how they reacted to the loss of their ministers and how they looked to the congregations of Mary's reign for their inspiration.

John Smith: – Indeed, as you said even now, for preaching and ministering the sacraments, so long as we might have the word freely preached, and the sacraments administered without the preferring of idolatrous gear above it, we never assembled together in houses. But when it came to this point, that all our preachers were displaced by your law, that would not subscribe to your apparel and your law, so that we could not hear none of them in any church by the space of seven or eight weeks, except Father Coverdale, of whom we have a good opinion; and yet (God knoweth) the man was so fearful, that he durst not be known unto us where he preached, though we sought it at his house. And then were we troubled and commanded to your courts from day to day, for not coming to our parish churches. Then we bethought us what were best to do; and we remembered that there was a congregation of us in this city in Queen Mary's days; and a congregation at Geneva, which used a book and order of preaching, ministering of the sacraments and discipline, most agreeable to the word of God; which book is allowed by that godly and well-learned man, Master Calvin, and the preachers there; which book and order we now hold. And if you can reprove this book, or anything that we hold, by the word of God, we will yield to you, and do open penance at Paul's Cross; if not, we will stand to it by the grace of God.
Bishop Grindal: – This is no answer.

Nicholson, W. (ed.), *The Remains of Edmund Grindal*, Parker Society, 1843, pp. 205–6.

document 26

The Pope excommmunicates Elizabeth, 1570

These are extracts from the papal bull excommunicating the Queen and releasing her Catholic subjects from any requirement of obedience to her.

He that reigneth on high, to whom is given all power in heaven and in earth, hath committed his one, holy, Catholic and apostolic church, out of which there is no salvation, to one alone upon earth, namely to Peter, the chief of the apostles, and to Peter's successor, the bishop of Rome, to be by him governed with plenary authority. Him alone hath he made prince over all people and all kingdoms. . . In discharge of which function, we, who are by God's goodness called to the government of the aforesaid church, do spare no pains, labouring with all earnestness, that unity and the Catholic religion . . . might be preserved sincere. But the number of the ungodly hath gotten such power, that there is now no place in the whole world left which they have not essayed to corrupt with their most wicked doctrines; and amongst others, Elizabeth, the pretended queen of England, the servant of wickedness, lendeth thereunto her helping hand, with whom, as in a sanctuary, the most pernicious persons have found a refuge. This very woman, having seized on the kingdom, and monstrously usurped the place of supreme head of the church in all England, and the chief authority and jurisdiction thereof, hath again reduced the said kingdom into a miserable and ruinous condition, which was so lately reclaimed to the Catholic faith and a thriving condition . . . we seeing that impieties and wicked actions are multiplied one upon the other, as also that the persecution of the faithful and affliction of religion groweth every day heavier and heavier, through the instigation and by the means of the said Elizabeth, and since we understand her heart to be so hardened and obdurate . . . are constrained of necessity to betake ourselves to the weapons of justice against her, being heartily grieved and sorry, that we are compelled thus to punish one to whose ancestors the whole state of Christendom hath been so much beholden . . . we do, out of the fulness of our apostolic power, declare the aforesaid Elizabeth, as being an heretic and favourer of heretics, and her adherents in the

matters aforesaid, to have incurred the sentence of excommunication, and to be cut off from the unity of the body of Christ. And
moreover we do declare her to be deprived of her pretended title
to the kingdom aforesaid, and of all dominion, dignity, and privilege whatsoever. . . And we do command and charge all and every
the noblemen, subjects, people, and others aforesaid, that they
presume not to obey her, or her orders, mandates and laws: and
those which shall do the contrary, we do include them in the like
sentence of anathema. *ex communicate them too!*

(**6**), pp. 416–8.

document 27

An Admonition to Parliament, 1572

Unlike the complaints of Colet and Latimer, this call for the removal of
abuses in the Church was addressed not to Convocation but to Parliament.
It demanded the removal of the 'lordly bishops' and a more equal preaching
ministry in the Church.

These and a great meanie other abuses ar in the ministerie remai-
nyng, which unlesse they be removed and the truth brought in, not
onely Gods justice shal be powred forth, but also Gods church in
this realme shall never be builded. . . The way therefore to avoid
these inconveniences, and to reforme these deformities is this: Your
wisedomes have to remove Advousons, Patronages, Impropri-
ations, and the bishoppes authoritie, claiming to themselves thereby
right to ordayne ministers, and to bryng in that old and true elec-
tion, which was accustomed to be made by the congregation. You
must displace those ignorant and unable ministers already placed,
& in their rowmes appoint such as both can, and wil by Gods
assistance feed the flock. . . Appoint to every congregation a
learned and diligent preacher. Remove homilies, articles, injunctions, a prescript order of service made out of the masse booke.
Take away the Lordship, the loyteryng, the pompe, the idlenes,
and livinges of Bishops, but yet employ them to such ends as they
were in the olde churche apointed for. Let a lawful and a godly
Seignorie loke that they preach, not quarterly or monthly, but
continually: not for fylthy lucre sake, but of a ready mynde. So God
shal be glorified, your consciences discharged, and the flocke of
Christ (purchased with his owne blood) edified. . .

Now then, if you wyl restore the church to his ancient officers, this you must doe. In stead of an Archbishop or Lord bishop, you must make equalitie of ministers. Instead of Chancelours . . . and such like: you have to plant . . . a lawful and godly seignorie. The Deaconship must not be confounded with the ministerie. . . . And to these three jointly, that is, the Ministers, Seniors, and deacons, is the whole regiment of the church to be committed. This regiment consisteth especially in ecclesiastical discipline, which is an order left by God unto his church, wherby men learne to frame their wylles and doyngs acordyng to the law of God, by instructing and admonishing one another, yea and by correcting and punishing all wylfull persones, and contemners of the same.

Frere, W. H. and Douglas, C. E., *Puritan Manifestos*, London, 1907, pp. 12–13, 16.

document 28
A warning to the bishops, 1572

The bishops responded to the Admonition *with a reply of their own, and this produced a further pamphlet from the Puritans to which these verses were added as a preface. It illustrates the widening gap between the establishment and the Puritans within the Elizabethan Church.*

TO THE PRELACIE

If men be dumbe, sure stones shall speake,
God wil his truthe prevaile,
Let men resist, it forceth not,
It standes when they shall quaile.

When it of men is most opprest,
Then God doth set in foote,
You Prelates knowe how true this is,
Thinke then what best may boote.

You that can councell other men,
Yourselves be councelled,
God will correct you knowe it well,
Where it is well deserved.

Yeelde reason why (none good you have)
Gods churche, Gods orders lacke,

Not God the cause, he them requires,
Your Lordships keepe them backe.

Thinke on the time reformde to be,
Your selves which chiefly ought,
You may else kicke, you wot who saith,
Its hard availing nought.

Repent, amende, shewe forth your love,
You which afflicte your owne,
And doe your best, while Antichriste
May quite be overthrowne.

By helpe of God, by helpe of Prince,
whome God long save and blesse,
With prosperous life, and earnest zeale,
At last heaven to possesse.

Frere, W. H. and Douglas, C. E., *Puritan Manifestos*, London, 1907, p. 78.

Bibliography

SOURCES

1 Brewer, J. S., Gardiner, J. and Brodie, R. H. (eds.), *The Letters and Papers of Henry VIII 1509–1547*, 21 vols, London, 1862–1932.

2 Brinkelow, H., *The Complaynt of Roderick Mors*, Early English Text Society, 1874.

3 Cardwell, E., *Synodalia*, Oxford, 1842.

4 Dasent, J. R., *Acts of the Privy Council of England and Wales*, 32 vols, London, 1890–1907.

5 Dickens, A. G. and Carr, D. (eds.), *The Reformation in England to the Accession of Elizabeth I*, Arnold, 1967.

6 Elton, G. R., *The Tudor Constitution*, Cambridge University Press, 2nd edn 1982.

7 Foxe, J., *Actes and Monuments of the English Church*, several editions and excerpts.

8 Frere, W. H. and Kennedy, W. P. M., *Visitation Articles and Injunctions of the Reformation Period*, 3 vols, Alcuin Club, 1910.

9 Gee, H. and Hardy, W. J., *Documents Illustrative of English Church History*, London, 1896.

10 Hanham, A., *The Churchwardens' Accounts of Ashburton 1479–1580*, Devon and Cornwall Record Society, 1970. (This and the next entry are excellent examples of the way in which local record societies have published documents relevant to the subject. It is impossible to list them all, but a search of the publications of local record societies is strongly recommended.)

11 Hodgett, G. A. J., *The State of the ex-religious and former chantry priests in the diocese of Lincoln*, Lincoln Record Society, 1959.

12 Hughes, P. L. and Larkin, J. F., *Tudor Royal Proclamations*, 3 vols, Yale University Press, 1964–1969.

13 Parker Society Publications. (A multi-volume series of the writings and letters of the sixteenth-century English reformers. When referred to, the particular volume is noted.)

14 *Statutes at Large,* Cambridge, 1762.
15 Strype, J., *Annals of the Reformation,* 4 vols, London, 1824 edn.
16 Strype, J., *Ecclesiastical Memorials,* 7 vols, London, 1816 edn.
17 Williams, C. H., *English Historical Documents 1485–1558,* Eyre & Spottiswoode, 1967.

BOOKS
18 Phythian-Adams, C., *The Desolation of a City: Coventry and the Urban Crisis of the Later Middle Ages,* Cambridge University Press, 1979.
19 Aston, M., *Lollards and Reformers: Images and Literacy in Late Medieval Religion,* Hambledon Press, 1984.
20 Aveling, H., *Northern Catholics,* Geoffrey Chapman, 1967.
21 Baskerville, G., *English Monks and the Suppression of the Monasteries,* Cape, 1940.
22 Booty, J. E., *John Jewel as Apologist of the Church of England,* S.P.C.K., 1963.
23 Bossy, J., *The English Catholic Community 1570–1850,* Darton, Longman and Todd, 1975.
24 Bowker, M., *The Secular Clergy in the Diocese of Lincoln 1495–1520,* Cambridge University Press, 1968.
25 Bowker, M., *The Henrician Reformation: the Diocese of Lincoln under John Longland 1521–1547,* Cambridge University Press, 1981.
26 Brook, V. J. K., *A Life of Archbishop Parker,* Clarendon Press, 1962.
27 Brooks, P. N., *Thomas Cranmer's Doctrine of the Eucharist; an essay in historical development,* Macmillan, 1965.
28 Chambers, R. W., *Thomas More,* Cape, 1935.
29 Clark, P., *English Provincial Society from the Reformation to the Revolution: Religion, Politics and Society in Kent 1500–1640,* Harvester Press, 1977.
30 Clark, P. and Slack, P., *English Towns in Transition 1500–1700,* Oxford University Press, 1976.
31 Clebsch, W., *England's Earliest Protestants 1520–35,* Yale University Press, 1964.
32 Collinson, P., *Archbishop Grindal 1519–1583,* Cape, 1979.
33 Collinson, P., *The Elizabethan Puritan Movement,* Cape, 1967.
34 Collinson, P., *Godly People: Essays on English Protestantism and Puritanism,* Hambledon Press, 1983.
35 Collinson, P., *The Religion of Protestants,* Oxford University Press, 1982.

Bibliography

36 Cornwell, J., *The Revolt of the Peasantry 1549*, Routledge & Kegan Paul, 1977.

37 Cross, M. C., *Church and People*, Fontana, 1976.

38 Cross, M. C., *The Puritan Earl; the life of Henry Hastings, third Earl of Huntingdon 1536–1595*, Macmillan, 1966.

39 Cross, M. C., *The Royal Supremacy in the Elizabethan Church*, Allen & Unwin, 1969.

40 Davies, H., *Worship and Theology in England from Cranmer to Hooker 1534–1603*, Princeton University Press, 1970.

41 Davis, J. F., *Heresy and Reformation in the South East of England, 1520–1559*, Royal Historical Society, 1983.

42 Dickens, A. G., *The English Reformation*, Batsford, 1964.

43 Dickens, A. G., *Lollards and Protestants in the Diocese of York 1509–1558*, Oxford University Press, 1959.

44 Dugmore, C. W., *The Mass and the English Reformers*, Macmillan, 1958.

45 Dures, A., *English Catholicism 1558–1642*, Longman, 1983.

46 Elton, G. R., *Policy and Police: the Enforcement of the Reformation in the Age of Thomas Cromwell*, Cambridge University Press, 1972.

47 Elton, G. R., *Reform and Reformation: England 1509–1558*, Arnold, 1977.

48 Elton, G. R., *Reform and Renewal: Thomas Cromwell and the Common Weal*, Cambridge University Press, 1973.

49 Fenlon, D., *Heresy and Obedience in Tridentine Italy*, Cambridge University Press, 1972.

50 Finch, M. E., *Five Northamptonshire Families*, Northants. Record Society, 1956.

51 Fletcher, A., *Tudor Rebellions*, 3rd edn., Longman, 1983.

52 Frere, W. H., *The English Church in the reigns of Elizabeth and James I*, Macmillan, 1904.

53 Garrett, C. H., *The Marian Exiles: a study in the Origins of English Protestantism*, Cambridge University Press, 1938.

54 Guy, J. A., *The Public Career of Sir Thomas More*, Harvester Press, 1980.

55 Haigh, C., *Reformation and Resistance in Tudor Lancashire*, Cambridge University Press, 1975.

56 Haigh, C. (ed.), *The Reign of Elizabeth I*, Macmillan, 1984.

57 Haller, W., *Foxe's Book of Martyrs and the Elect Nation*, Cape, 1963.

58 Haugaard, W., *Elizabeth and the English Reformation*, Cambridge University Press, 1968.

59 Heal, F. M. and O'Day, R., *Church and Society in England: Henry VIII to James I*, Macmillan, 1977.

60 Heal, F. M. and O'Day, R., *Princes and Paupers in the English Church 1500–1800*, Leicester University Press, 1981.

61 Heal, F., *Of Prelates and Princes: a Study of the Economic and Social Position of the Tudor Episcopate*, Cambridge University Press, 1980.

62 Heath, P., *The English Parish Clergy on the Eve of the Reformation*, Routledge & Kegan Paul, 1969.

63 Hopf, C., *Martin Bucer and the English Reformation*, Blackwell, 1946.

64 Houlbrooke, R., *Church Courts and People during the English Reformation 1520–1570*, Oxford University Press, 1979.

65 Hudson, W. S., *Cambridge and the Elizabethan Settlement of 1559*, Duke University Press, 1980.

66 James, M. E., *Family, Lineage and Civil Society: A Study of the Durham Region 1500–1640*, Oxford University Press, 1974.

67 Jones, N. L., *Faith by Statute: Parliament and the Settlement of Religion 1559*, Royal Historical Society, 1982.

68 Jones, W. R. D., *The Tudor Commonwealth 1529–1559*, Athlone Press, 1970.

69 Jordan, W. K., *Edward VI; the Young King*, Allen & Unwin, 1968.

70 Jordan, W. K., *Edward VI; the Threshold of Power*, Allen & Unwin, 1970.

71 Jordan, W. K., *The Charities of Rural England*, Allen & Unwin, 1961.

72 Knowles, D. M., *The Religious Orders in England: iii, The Tudor Age*, Cambridge University Press, 1959.

73 Krieder, A., *The English Chantries: the Road to Dissolution*, Harvard University Press, 1979.

74 Lehmberg, S. E., *The Reformation Parliament 1529–1536*, Cambridge University Press, 1970.

75 Lehmberg, S. E., *The Later Parliaments of the Reign of Henry VIII*, Cambridge University Press, 1980.

76 Loach, J. and Tittler, R., *The Mid-Tudor Polity c. 1540–1560*, Macmillan, 1980.

77 Loades, D. M., *The Oxford Martyrs*, Batsford, 1967.

78 Loades, D. M., *The Reign of Mary Tudor*, Benn, 1981.

79 McCaffrey, W. C., *The Shaping of the Elizabethan Regime*, Princeton University Press, 1968.

Bibliography

80 McConica, J. K., *English Humanists and Reformation Politics under Henry VIII and Edward VI*, Clarendon Press, 1965.

81 MacLure, M., *The Paul's Cross Sermons 1534–1642*, Toronto University Press, 1958.

82 Manning, R. G., *Religion and Society in Elizabethan Sussex*, Leicester University Press, 1969.

83 Mingay, G. E., *The Gentry: the Rise and Fall of a Ruling Class*, Longman, 1976.

84 Mozley, J. F., *William Tyndale*, S.P.C.K., 1937.

85 Mozley, J. F., *Coverdale and his Bibles*, S.P.C.K., 1953.

86 Mommsen, W. J., *et al.*, *The Urban Classes, The Nobility and the Reformation*, German Historical Institute, 1979.

87 Muller, J. A., *Stephen Gardiner and the Tudor Reaction*, S.P.C.K., 1926.

88 Neale, J. E., *Elizabeth I and Her Parliaments 1559–1581*, Cape, 1953.

89 O'Day, R. and Heal, F. M., *Continuity and Change: Personnel and Administration of the Church of England 1500–1642*, Leicester University Press, 1976.

90 Orme, N., *Education in the West of England 1066–1548*, Exeter University Press, 1976.

91 Owen, D. M., *Religion and Society in Medieval Lincolnshire*, Lincolnshire Local History Society, 1971.

92 Oxley, J., *The Reformation in Essex to the Death of Mary*, Manchester University Press, 1968.

93 Palmer, M. D., *Henry VIII*, Longman, 1971.

94 Palliser, D. M., *Tudor York*, Oxford University Press, 1979.

95 Parmiter, G. de C., *The King's Great Matter*, Longman, 1967.

96 Scott-Pearson, F., *Thomas Cartwright and Elizabethan Puritanism*, Cambridge University Press, 1926.

97 Pollard, A. F., *Wolsey*, Collins, 1929.

98 Porter, H. C., *Reformation and Reaction in Tudor Cambridge*, Cambridge University Press, 1958.

99 Read, C., *Mr. Secretary Cecil and Queen Elizabeth*, Cape, 1955.

100 Richardson, W. C., *A History of the Court of Augmentations 1536–1554*, Louisiana State University Press, 1961.

101 Ridley, J., *Thomas Cranmer*, Oxford University Press, 1962.

102 Scarisbrick, J. J., *Henry VIII*, Eyre & Spottiswoode, 1968.

103 Scarisbrick, J. J., *The Reformation and the English People*, Blackwell, 1984.

104 Sheils, W. J., *The Puritans in the Diocese of Peterborough 1570–1610*, Northants. Record Society, 1979.

105 Hassell-Smith, A., *County and Court: Government and Politics in Norfolk 1558–1603*, Oxford University Press, 1974.

106 Smith, R. B., *Land and Politics in the England of Henry VIII: the West Riding of Yorkshire 1530–1546*, Clarendon Press, 1970.

107 Tawney, R. H., *Religion and the Rise of Capitalism*, Penguin edn., 1938.

108 Thomas, K., *Religion and the Decline of Magic*, Penguin edn., 1973.

109 Thomson, J. A. F., *The Later Lollards 1414–1520*, Oxford University Press, 1965.

110 Vale, M. G. A., *Piety, Charity and Literacy among the Yorkshire Gentry 1370–1480*, Borthwick Papers, 1976.

111 Wernham, R. B., *Before the Armada; the Growth of English Foreign Policy*, Cape, 1966.

112 Wilkie, W. E., *The Cardinal Protectors of England: Rome and the Tudors before the Reformation*, Cambridge University Press, 1974.

113 Wilson, D., *A Tudor Tapestry: Men, Women and Society in Reformation England*, Heinemann, 1972.

114 Youings, J., *The Dissolution of the Monasteries*, Allen & Unwin, 1971.

ARTICLES
The following abbreviations are used:

EcHR	*Economic History Review*
EHR	*English Historical Review*
HJ	*Historical Journal*
JEH	*Journal of Ecclesiastical History*
P&P	*Past and Present*
SCH	*Studies in Church History*
TBGAS	*Transactions of the Bristol and Gloucestershire Archaeological Society*
TRHS	*Transactions of the Royal Historical Society*

115 Phythian-Adams, C., 'Ceremony and the Citizen: the Communal Year at Coventry 1450–1550', in Clark, P. and Slack, P., (eds) *Crisis and Order in English Towns*, 1972.

116 Alexander, G., 'Bonner and the Marian Persecutions', *History*, 60, 1975.

117 Bowker, M., 'The Supremacy and the Episcopate: The Struggle for Control 1534–1540', *HJ*, 18, 1975.

118 Bradshaw, B., 'The Controversial Sir Thomas More', *JEH*, 36, 1985.

119 Brigden, S., 'Popular Disturbance and the Fall of Thomas Cromwell and the Reformers, 1539–1540', *HJ*, 24, 1981.

120 Brigden, S., 'Tithe Controversy in Reformation London', *JEH*, 32, 1981.

121 Brigden, S., 'Youth and the English Reformation', *P&P*, 95, 1982.

122 Burgess, C., '"For the increase of divine service": Chantries and the Parish in late-medieval Bristol', *JEH*, 36, 1985.

123 Cross, M. C., 'Parochial Structure and the Dissemination of Protestantism in 16th century England: a tale of two cities', *SCH*, 16, 1979.

124 Dowling, M., 'Anne Boleyn and Reform', *JEH*, 35, 1984.

125 Habbakuk, H. J., 'The Market for Monastic Property', *EcHR*, 2 series, 10, 1958.

126 Haigh, C., 'Anti-clericalism and the English Reformation', *History*, 68, 1983.

127 Haigh, C., 'The Continuity of Catholicism in the English Reformation', *P&P*, 93, 1981.

128 Heath, P., 'Staffordshire Towns and the Reformation', *North Staffordshire Journal of Field Studies*, 19, 1979.

129 Houlbrooke, R. A., 'Persecution of Heresy and Protestantism in the Diocese of Norwich under Henry VIII', *Norfolk Archaeology*, 35, 1973.

130 Kelly, M., 'The Submission of the Clergy', *TRHS*, 1965.

131 Loades, D. M., 'The Last Years of Cuthbert Tunstall 1547–1559', *Durham University Journal*, 66, 1973.

132 Martin, J. W., 'The Protestant Underground Congregations of Mary's Reign', *JEH*, 35, 1984.

133 McGrath, P., 'Elizabethan Catholicism: a Reconsideration', *JEH*, 35, 1984.

134 Mayhew, G., 'Religion, Faction and Politics in Reformation Rye: 1530–1559', *Sussex Archaeological Collections*, 120, 1982.

135 Powell, K. G., 'The Beginnings of Protestantism in Gloucestershire', *TBGAS*, 90, 1971.

136 Powell, K. G., 'The Social Background to the Reformation in Gloucestershire', *TBGAS*, 92, 1973.

137 Price, F. D., 'Gloucester Diocese under Bishop Hooper 1551–3' *TBGAS*, 60, 1938.

138 Redworth, G., 'A Study in the Formulation of Policy: the Genesis and Evolution of the Act of Six Articles', *JEH*, 37, 1986.

139 Scarisbrick, J. J., 'The Pardon of the Clergy, 1531', *Cambridge Historical Journal*, 12, 1956.

140 Tudor, P., 'Religious Instruction for Children and Adolescents in the Early English Reformation', *JEH*, 35, 1984.

141 Whiting, R., '"Abominable Idols": Image and Image-Breaking under Henry VIII', *JEH*, 33, 1982.

142 Whiting, R., '"For the Health of my Soul": Prayers for the Dead in the Tudor South-West', *Southern History*, 3, 1984.

143 Zell, M., 'The Personnel of the Clergy in Kent during the Reformation', *EHR*, 89, 1974.

Index

Index